JOURNEYING THROUGH THE YEAR OF MATTHEW

In memory of

My sister, Louise Keating (née Littleton),
Who died on 23 March 2010, aged 46 years,

and

My father, Johnny Littleton,
Who died on 15 May 2010, aged 86 years.

May they rest in peace.

John Littleton

Journeying through the Year of Matthew
Reflections on the Gospel

the columba press

First published in 2010 by
the columba press
55A Spruce Avenue, Stillorgan Industrial Park,
Blackrock, Co Dublin

Cover by Bill Bolger
Origination by The Columba Press
Printed in Ireland by ColourBooks Ltd, Dublin

ISBN 978 1 85607 724 8

Acknowledgements
Biblical quotations are from *The Jerusalem Bible*, copyright © 1966, 1967 and 1968 Darton, Longman and Todd, and Doubleday and Co Inc. All rights reserved. Used by permission.

Contents

Preface

The Gospel is Good News and the purpose of this book is to provide readers with an overview of the Gospel according to Matthew, which is proclaimed during Year A of the Church's liturgical cycle. After introducing some of the principal themes of Matthew's Gospel, a series of reflections on the gospel readings is presented for each Sunday and major feast during the year.

The reflections focus on the relevance of Matthew's Gospel for everyday life and will be helpful to priests and laity wishing to engage more fully with the word of God. They will be particularly useful to members of prayer groups, Bible-study classes and *lectio divina* gatherings preparing for the celebration of the Liturgy of the Word during the Sunday liturgy. A helpful appendix at the end of the book indicates the order for the gospel readings for the Sundays in Ordinary time.

The reflections form the substantial part of the book. Before each one, the reference for the relevant gospel reading is listed. Then after each reflection, a suitable phrase or short passage from the gospel is offered as an aid to personal prayer and meditation.

The scripture quotations throughout the book are taken from *The Jerusalem Bible* which, regrettably in some instances, does not employ gender-inclusive language, because that is the version of the scriptures that is generally used in lectionaries and, as such, the version with which most people are familiar.

While the reflections may be read without necessarily referring to the gospel texts, it is recommended that readers also use their Bibles or missals. Otherwise, individual gospel phrases could be taken out of context. Also, because the word of God is inexhaustible, it is impossible to be totally comprehensive in any given reflection. Hopefully, the reflections presented here will inspire readers to develop their own thoughts on the Gospel of Matthew.

Finally, earlier versions of some of the reflections were published in *The Catholic Times* and in the *Tipperary Star*, and an earlier version of the introductory essay was published in *Scripture in Church*.

INTRODUCTION

Jesus Christ:
The Fulfilment of the Law and the Prophets

On most Sundays (except during Lent and Easter, when the readings are chosen from the Gospel according to John) and on quite a few of the more significant feasts during Year A of the three-year liturgical cycle, we listen to extracts from the Gospel according to Matthew being proclaimed in our celebrations of the Eucharist, and we ponder the implications of Matthew's message for everyday Christian living. Thus we are doing exactly what the pilgrim People of God are called to do: we are journeying towards our true and final destiny (that is, heaven), while being guided, encouraged and challenged by the wisdom and lessons of Matthew's Gospel.

Gospel: Good News for Believers
The Gospel of Matthew, like those of Mark, Luke and John, is indeed Good News, even though, according to Seán P. Kealy, 'Matthew does not have Mark's vivid realism, Luke's sheer gentle beauty or John's lofty mysticism'.[1] Matthew's Gospel was most probably written during the decade 80-90AD and, now as then, is intended to offer Christians hope as they are confronted by the various trials and tribulations of life. In this context, we need to understand that Matthew's Gospel, like other biblical books, is not primarily an historical document providing readers with accurate biographical information, facts and figures about Jesus of Nazareth (although, undoubtedly, it contains some historical details).

Instead, Matthew's Gospel is first and foremost a faith document that was written post-Calvary for the spiritual benefits of those who, having become believers in the Risen Christ, had

1. Seán P. Kealy, 'On reading Matthew', *Scripture in Church*, 26 (103), 1996, p 348

committed themselves to his teaching and example. Scripture scholars often describe the gospels as having been written through 'Resurrection-tinted spectacles', implying that the evangelists worked from the particular perspective of belief in the Risen Lord. Therefore, the Gospel of Matthew, like the other three gospels, is essentially a faith document that bears witness to the Resurrection, thereby acknowledging that Jesus is Lord and that, having been raised from the dead, he is alive and active in the Christian community which is animated by his abiding presence (see Mt 18:20; 28:20). Philip Fogarty confirms this principle when he argues that 'the purpose of the gospels was, above all, to engender a response of faith and to bring salvation'.[2]

Matthew: What is Distinctive?

The Gospel according to Matthew is effectively a major reworking of the earlier Mark's Gospel, incorporating the vast majority of verses (600 of 661) from Mark. Moreover, Matthew's Gospel includes an infancy narrative, thus making it more a pseudo-biography of Jesus than Mark's Gospel. Matthew's stories about the birth of Jesus – especially the wise men travelling from the east (see Mt 2:1), the significance of Bethlehem as a location (see Mt 2:6), the flight into Egypt (see Mt 2:14-15) and the settling in Nazareth (see Mt 2:23) – emphasise the messianic and divine status of Jesus. So, in a sense, geography is at the service of theology.

Although Matthew's Gospel has much in common with the other gospels, especially the other two synoptics,[3] it also has some unique characteristics. Central to these is the Jewish-Christian community for whom it was most likely written. And because this gospel was written predominantly for Christians with a Jewish background, it frequently refers to the Hebrew

2. Philip Fogarty, *According to Matthew*, Dublin: Messenger Publications, 2007, p 5

3. The Gospels of Matthew, Mark and Luke are usually referred to as the synoptic gospels or synoptics (from the Greek *syn*, meaning together, and *opsis*, meaning appearance) because they share many common parables and accounts in addition to a general agreement on the sequence of events.

scriptures and to the fulfilment of their prophecies in and through Jesus.[4]

Therefore, the Gospel according to Matthew presents Jesus as the new Moses, who liberates his people from slavery to sin. Hence, for example, the focus on the genealogy of Jesus at the beginning (see Mt 1:1-17), and the parallel between Jesus' preaching of the Beatitudes on the hill (see Mt 5:1-12) and Moses' reception of the Ten Commandments (also known as the Decalogue) on Mount Sinai (see Exod 20:1-17). But Jesus is not merely another Moses, although Moses was unquestionably the greatest leader of the Israelites.

According to Matthew's Gospel, Jesus is the fulfilment of the Torah and the Prophets, the realisation of God's promise to send the Messiah. Not surprisingly, then, Jesus said unambiguously: 'Do not imagine that I have come to abolish the Law or the Prophets. I have come not to abolish but to complete them' (Mt 5:17). That is why Jesus regularly referred to the established Jewish norms and customs, and then proceeded to claim that his teaching transcended them. Jesus is the Messiah who inaugurated the rule (or kingdom) of God here on earth.

Prophecy and Fulfilment

To appreciate this, we must understand that Matthew devised the notion of an inextricable link between prophecy and fulfil-ment, as if it were intrinsic to prophecy that it has a future di-mension. Crucially, this reference to the future was not inherent to the activity of prophecy, which was really concerned with 'speaking out' on behalf of God in the present – although the prophets also warned the people about future punishment if God's commandments were not obeyed, but in the context of the present. Matthew portrayed the major events in Jesus' life as if they were in a prophecy-fulfilment arrangement. For exam-ple, in Matthew's infancy narrative, we read five times: 'this was to fulfil what the Lord had spoken through the prophet' (Mt 1:22; 2:5; 2:15; 2:17; 2:23).

By doing this, Matthew added a future orientation to

---

4. See Donald Senior, *What are they saying about Matthew?* New York: Paulist Press, 1983, pp 37-46

prophecy that it did not originally have. However, Matthew's purpose in doing so was to reassure those Jewish people who had begun to recognise Jesus as the Messiah that the path they were following was closely related to the events of the Hebrew Bible. In this way, the Gospel according to Matthew countered the judgement of the Jewish religious authorities that any Jews who accepted Jesus as the Messiah or, worse, as the Son of God, were not only separating themselves from the traditions of Israel but from the God of Israel too. As Donald Senior suggests, 'like skilled preachers, the evangelists told their stories of Jesus in such a way that they would touch the concerns and hopes of their audience'.[5]

Significantly, Matthew's Gospel changed the Markan phrase 'kingdom of God' to 'kingdom of heaven', considering that Mark's copious use of the name God was too irreverent. This suggests again that the Gospel of Matthew was written for those who belonged to the particular strand of the Jewish tradition which emphasised the transcendence of God rather than his immanence.[6]

There are several other noteworthy distinctions between the Gospel of Matthew and the other gospels. Rob Esdaile has summarised them:[7]

- the infancy description of the visit of the Magi (see Mt 2:1-12);
- the flight into Egypt and the murder of the Innocents (see Mt 2:13-23);
- the longer form of the Beatitudes (see Mt 5:3-12) [see also Lk 6:20-23];
- the Matthean antitheses (see Mt 5:21-47);
- the best-known version of the Lord's Prayer (see Mt 6:9-15) [see also Lk 11:1-4];
- the invitation to the overburdened to seek rest (see Mt 11:28-30);

---

5. Donald Senior, *What are they saying about Matthew?* p 5
6. The transcendence of God refers to the otherness of God whose existence goes beyond the universe and is not to be identified with it. The immanence of God refers to God's presence everywhere and in everything.
7. See Rob Esdaile, 'A Year with Matthew', *The Pastoral Review*, 3 (6), 2007, p 13

- the parables of the hidden treasure, the pearl and the dragnet (see Mt 13:44-50);
- the more detailed account of Peter's confession (see Mt 16:16-19) [see also Jn 6:69];
- the parables of the unforgiving debtor, the vineyard labourers, the two sons, and the sheep and the goats (see Mt 18:23-35; 20:1-16; 21:28-32; 25:31-46).

The Sermon on the Mount

The Sermon on the Mount (see Mt 5-7), which begins with the Beatitudes, is pivotal to the Gospel of Matthew because it enunciates Jesus' ethical teaching. It is a marvellous example of how Jesus understood the development of the old covenant in the new. That development was expressed by Jesus when he spoke about 'these words of mine' (Mt 7:24, 26) implying that his words went beyond those of the Ten Commandments. Accordingly, it is no longer sufficient to adhere to the external law, so to speak, because God looks into the heart and his people are now ready to understand that. It is no longer adequate not to kill another person. Now people must learn to control the anger that leads to such killing. Neither is it enough not to commit adultery. People must now learn to control their senses and discipline the desires that lead to adultery. In this way, Matthew's Gospel still challenges us to 'do the will of [the] Father in heaven' (Mt 7:21) and to 'be perfect just as [our] heavenly Father is perfect' (Mt 5:48).

Peter and the Church

Notably, Matthew's Gospel, which is often known as the Gospel of the Church, reveals Peter's unique leadership role. Because of the faith he professed in Christ, Peter was personally appointed to lead the emerging Church. Peter was given a key position of authority in the Church (which Catholics now call the Papacy). While Jesus told Peter that the reason he was able to recognise Jesus' divinity was because he was specially graced by God (see Mt 16:17), Jesus also rebuked him for opposing his passion. On the one hand, Jesus gave Peter the keys of the kingdom (see Mt 16:19), whereas, on the other hand, he said, 'Get behind me, Satan! You are an obstacle in my path, because the way you think is not God's way but [human]' (Mt 16:23). This is a reminder that Peter, like us, was weak and fickle. Peter was appointed by Christ to lead his Church, but Peter was not impeccable. He was a weak human being who, nevertheless, was used by God to build up the Church on earth.

Conclusion: the Journey Motif in Matthew's Gospel
Matthew's Gospel adopts the journey motif found in Mark's Gospel and records Jesus' journeys. He began his public ministry in Galilee and travelled towards Jerusalem. Significantly, it could be argued that there is a certain symbolism here: the journey was not only geographical but was really symbolic of Jesus' return to the Father.[8] Once more, it could be claimed that geography is at the service of theology.

Matthew's Gospel is a reinterpretation of the Torah for Jewish Christians. The role of the modern reader is to reinterpret Matthew for today, in each new geographical and historical era, just as the Old Testament prophets did with the Torah. A meditative reading of the text of Matthew will help to make sense of the implications of Matthew's message for everyday Christian living.

Recommended Reading
Christ, Jennifer, *Journeying with Matthew: five minute preparation for each Sunday liturgy*, New York: Paulist Press, 2007

Esdaile, Rob, 'A year with Matthew', *The Pastoral Review*, 3 (6), 2007, pp 12-16

Fogarty, Philip, *According to Matthew*, Dublin: Messenger Publications, 2007

Harrington, Wilfrid J., *Matthew – sage theologian: the Jesus of Matthew*, Dublin: The Columba Press, 1988

Kealy, Seán P., 'On reading Matthew', *Scripture in Church*, 26 (103), 1996, pp 348-352

Senior, Donald, *What are they saying about Matthew?* New York: Paulist Press, 1983

---

8. This reminds us of the quest that is at the heart of Christianity.

The Season of Advent

First Sunday of Advent
Gospel reading: Matthew 24:37-44

Reflection
Christmas begins earlier every year in the secular world. Many shops and businesses compete to have the first and the biggest display of Christmas lights and decorations. Advertisements for Christmas toys commence in October. People are posting Christmas cards before the end of November and children are taken to visit Santa Claus early in December. Therefore, it is not surprising that some people feel that Christmas is an anticlimax because it has ended almost before it has begun.

In the Christian context, however, and especially in the liturgical year, Christmas does not begin until 25 December and it is preceded by several weeks of waiting and preparation during the season of Advent. Our focus in Advent is on waiting in hope for the fulfilment of God's promise to send the Messiah and on preparing for the Second Coming of Christ on the Last Day when all the nations will be assembled before him.

Our Christian hope is incomplete without this understanding of Advent. Advent is not just about preparing to commemorate the birth of the baby Jesus. Crucially, it is a time of spiritual preparation for welcoming Christ into our lives at Christmas, but also a time of preparation for the last judgement. Basically, during Advent the Church invites us not to be lured into a false sense of Christmas that is unrelated to the real meaning of Christmas, which is the Incarnation, that is, God becoming human in the person of Jesus, and to Christ's Second Coming. The season of Advent begins today.

Advent is the great season of hope in the Church's liturgical year. Thus we are challenged to be hope-filled people awaiting the Lord's coming into our lives and into the world. However, there is an important difference between the secular and Christian understandings of hope.

The secular sense of hope, which is most accurately expressed as wishful thinking, lacks surety or certainty. To be hopeful in the secular sense is to articulate a desire or a wish that may or may not be realised. For example, when we say, 'We hope that our business will not become bankrupt', our wish is for success in business but we cannot be certain that there will be success.

In sharp contrast, Christian hope is a virtue and it expresses certainty based on God's promise to be faithful to us in all circumstances. For instance, when we say, 'We hope in the resurrection of the dead', we are not simply engaging in wishful thinking. We are articulating and communicating a certainty that is based on our faith.

Jesus told his disciples: 'You too must stand ready because the Son of Man is coming at an hour you do not expect' (Mt 24:44). He says the same to each one of us. In doing so, he exhorts us to make this particular Advent the beginning of a lifelong Advent – a lifetime of waiting in Christian hope for the Lord's Second Coming, whenever that will be, while undergoing conversion from sin to living in God's presence.

We hope for the Lord's coming. This means that, as Christians, we are sure that he is coming. There is no doubt. The season of Advent provides us with an annual opportunity to deepen our waiting in hope for the realisation of God's saving promise in Jesus Christ our Lord and Saviour.

For meditation
So stay awake, because you do not know the day when your master is coming. (Mt 24:42)

Second Sunday of Advent
Gospel reading: Matthew 3:1-12

Reflection

John the Baptist was the last in a long line of prophets who foretold the coming of the Messiah. He prepared the way for the Messiah by alerting God's people to the Messiah's impending arrival and by challenging them to change their lives by repenting for their sins. A radical abandonment of sinful living was required because God was going to communicate with his people directly through his Son, Jesus, the Messiah.

John's ministry focused on preaching conversion and proclaiming a baptism of repentance for the forgiveness of sin. Repentance is a fundamental change of heart, or attitude, which results in leaving sin behind and embracing God's freely shared life and love. Such change is only possible with the gift of God's grace. There was urgency in John's preaching about repentance. The time for repentance, he said, is now, not in the future. Repentance through prayer, fasting and charitable works leads to conversion, and conversion is an important aspect of people's preparation if they are to meet Christ when he comes.

John understood from his own experience in the wilderness, where he spent a long time in prayer and reflection, that repentance and conversion were absolutely necessary. Otherwise their hearts would remain closed by sinful preoccupations and they would not be able to recognise the Messiah when he arrived. And, if they could not recognise him, neither would they be able to acknowledge him as the fulfilment of God's promise to liberate his people. Without a 'change-of-heart' (*metanoia* in the original Greek), a turning back towards God, there could be no appreciation of the Messiah's presence among them.

We learn from the gospels that John fasted and did penance, wore camel hair and ate locusts and wild honey. So there was a strong witness dimension in his efforts to prepare the way for Christ to come into the people's lives. He was courageous and unapologetic in how he spoke. This witness and courage provided him with great credibility and, consequently, many people felt invited to consider seriously the relevance of his message because they noticed how he had taken it to heart himself. But his preaching made him unpopular with some people because they could not accept the truth, and remained unrepentant.

In what ways are we repentant people? How do we demonstrate our sincerity as witnesses to the teaching of Christ and the Church? What does it mean to be courageous and unapologetic about our convictions? The reality is that some of us are unrepentant for our sins. We are reluctant to speak about our faith and share it with others. Advent challenges us to become people of hope and expectation as we await Christ's coming.

As we prepare for Christmas, how will we prepare ourselves and help others to prepare for the arrival of the Messiah? If we follow the example of John the Baptist, we will truly be Advent people.

For meditation
Repent, for the kingdom of heaven is close at hand. (Mt 3:2)

Third Sunday of Advent
Gospel reading: Matthew 11:2-11

Reflection

During Advent we are a people in waiting. Advent is a hope-filled time, a time of expectation and anticipation. But, most of all, it is a time of waiting: waiting for the Messiah to arrive in our lives and in the world. His first arrival, when he was born in a stable, may be commemorated at Christmas. Or his second arrival, when he will come as King and Judge on the Last day, may be anticipated. Or his daily coming into our lives, in prayer, people and activities, may be acknowledged.

Waiting is part of all our lives. However, if the time we spend waiting is to be useful, our waiting must be purposeful. This means that we must wait properly for people, events and outcomes, always using the time effectively and efficiently to prepare for them. If we do not, the time spent waiting is wasted. And, regrettably, there is so much wasted time in our lives.

An essential quality of purposeful or effective waiting is patience. For example, if we become impatient while waiting for retirement from work or for the school term to finish, we simply waste that time. Impatience leads to frustration, anxiety, anger, cynicism and, ultimately, unhappiness. Unhappiness prevents us from doing anything constructive to sustain and prepare us while we wait. Our waiting is in vain and, inevitably, we are not ready when the time finally comes.

Similarly, if we do not use these days of Advent properly by waiting patiently for Christ to come into our lives at Christmas – especially by recognising and welcoming him in the sacraments and in other people – then we will not be ready to meet him when he comes. Frustration, anxiety, anger and cynicism are alien to the hope-filled spirit of Advent.

We need to be patient as we wait for the Lord's arrival. When John the Baptist was in prison, having heard about Jesus' ministry, he sent his disciples to ask Jesus: 'Are you the one who is to come, or have we got to wait for somebody else?' (Mt 11:3). John was the last in a long line of prophets who had been waiting for generations for the Messiah to come.

John and his disciples were privileged but not all of them

realised that the Messiah had arrived even when Jesus sent this clear message to John: 'Go back and tell John what you hear and see; the blind see again, and the lame walk, lepers are cleansed, and the deaf hear, and the dead are raised to life and the Good News is proclaimed to the poor' (Mt 11:4-5).

The message of Advent, then, is that we should wait patiently for the Lord to come into our lives. Our waiting can be a time of enrichment during which some positive change occurs.

Even as we await Jesus' arrival at Christmas, he is present to us in word and sacrament. But he is also present to us in the words and gestures of other people, if only we would become more astute in recognising him. It is only when we are patient that we avoid the frustration prevalent in the lives of many people that, in turn, prevents them from being truly open to the presence and influence of Christ at Christmas.

For meditation
I tell you solemnly, of all the children born of women, a greater than John the Baptist has never been seen; yet the least in the kingdom of heaven is greater than he is. (Mt 11:11)

Fourth Sunday of Advent
Gospel reading: Matthew 1:18-24

Reflection

Joseph is someone about whom we know little. There are few references to him in the gospels apart from the stories about the birth, infancy and childhood of Jesus (see Mt 13:55 and the parallels in Mark and Luke). He is very much a secondary or background figure in the gospel story. Yet, he is a real Advent person because, in a truly humble and remarkable manner, he prepares for the arrival of the Messiah into his life and into the world.

Matthew presents Joseph as having had no part in Mary's pregnancy. When Joseph discovered that Mary was pregnant he wondered how this could be since they had not been living together as husband and wife. Initially he was confused and he did not know what to do. However, he did not act rashly. He listened to God's word through the angel's message in a dream and, although it demanded much faith, he did what God asked him. He allowed his life to be influenced and directed by God's will. Therefore, without complaining, Joseph decided to prepare for the birth of Jesus by caring about Mary during her pregnancy.

Thus two aspects of Joseph's character are revealed to us. First, Joseph was obviously a man of deep faith. He trusted God and, discerning God's will, took the great leap of faith into the unknown in a difficult and confusing situation. God moved him in strange ways and he was responsive to this. Secondly, Joseph was selfless. He did not alienate Mary but, instead, accepted her and remained loyal. His selflessness enabled him to act without fear of ridicule and scorn. Doing God's will was all-important for Joseph.

We can learn from these two aspects of Joseph's character. For example, how do we respond to God who often communicates with us in strange ways? Are we able to make the leap of faith when we are unsure about the future? Can we acknowledge and embrace those people and life situations which least suit us? Advent is about cultivating our ability to focus beyond our own concerns and respond to the needs of other people so that Christ can come into our lives through them.

Joseph, in the portrait painted of him in Matthew's Gospel,

prepared for the birth of Jesus with gentleness and faithfulness. He cherished and supported Mary and, together, they brought Christ into the world. Joseph's discernment of God's will empowered his confidence. We are challenged to imitate Joseph's example as we live and work with other people.

Joseph was a man of few words but decisive and significant actions. His behaviour made a difference. Unfortunately, some of us speak many words but these words are rendered meaningless by our contradictory behaviour. This can easily occur during the days of Christmas when we gather as families and friends. Therefore, let us learn from the example of Joseph. Let us discern and accept joyfully God's will in our lives. And let us pray to Joseph, asking him to help us to do God's will always.

For meditation
When Joseph woke up he did what the angel of the Lord had told him to do. (Mt 1:24)

The Season of Christmas

The Nativity of the Lord

Gospel reading (Vigil Mass): Matthew 1:1-25
Gospel reading (Midnight Mass): Luke 2:1-14
Gospel reading (Dawn Mass): Luke 2:15-20
Gospel reading (Mass during the Day): John 1:1-18

Reflection

Thankfully, many of us are lucky enough to open gifts every Christmas Day. These gifts are signs of respect, affection and love for the person or people to whom they are given. They are normally given without any conditions and, occasionally, they are important tokens of gratitude.

Christmas may be described as encapsulating several significant themes: for example, homecomings, festive celebrations and holidays from school and work. Nevertheless, it is fundamentally about the greatest gift that humankind could receive from God after the most basic gift of creation and life itself: the gift of redemption from the consequences of sin, which has entered the world and human history in the person of Jesus Christ, the Word made flesh.

It is always fascinating to watch young children opening their Christmas presents. They usually do so with great excitement and much impatience. In their eagerness to discover what gifts they have received, they often tear off the wrapping paper and packaging, casting them aside and disregarding them as if they were not part of the presents.

Although understandable, their enthusiasm is insensitive to the people who took so much care choosing appropriate wrapping paper and carefully folding the edges to ensure that the present looked perfect. No offence is ever taken, though, because adults love to see the innocence of childhood in such anticipation and excitement.

Basically, then, there is much more to giving a present than the gift itself that lies under several layers of wrapping. There is also the selection of suitable packaging and the extra care taken when parcelling. Frequently, too, there is the specially chosen card that has a significant message written on it. All these extra layers are as much part of the gift as what is found inside. But it is possible that their meaning is overlooked in the rush to get at the gift.

There is a crucial lesson here for us about how we welcome the newborn infant Jesus. He is the fulfilment of God's promise to send the Messiah. But his coming into the world was carefully choreographed by God the Father so that people would be properly prepared for his arrival. The various layers of wrapping are the details of the unfolding story of salvation history over many centuries.

For instance, Jesus, the gift of our heavenly Father, was carefully anticipated by the long series of Old Testament prophets, culminating in John the Baptist, who spoke faithfully about his impending arrival and challenged the people to undergo repentance for their sins. Similarly, Jesus' birth was heralded to the world by the angels who sang 'Glory to God in the highest heaven, and peace to people who enjoy his favour' (Lk 2:14).

Amidst the excitement and confusion associated with Jesus' birth, we learn that his mother, Mary, 'treasured all these things and pondered them in her heart' (Lk 2:19). She acknowledged that God had done great things in her life, as we recite in the famous *Magnificat* prayer (see Lk 1:46-55). None of the many layers of wrapping had gone unnoticed by the mother of Jesus. She never forgot the goodness of God and the tremendous blessing that he had given, not only to her but to his Chosen People.

As we go home from Mass today, let us remember to notice everything about the presents that we receive from those who love us. In thanking them, let us acknowledge their efforts in surrounding their gift with layers of love that are symbolised in the wrapping and packaging.

Then let us, like Mary the mother of Jesus, ponder the wonder of what God has done for the human race by sending his only Son among us to save us from our sins. In doing so, let us recognise how God deliberately, carefully and lovingly prepared the world and its people for this great day.

For meditation
No one has ever seen God; it is the only Son, who is nearest to the Father's heart, who has made him known. (Jn 1:18)

The Holy Family of Jesus, Mary and Joseph
Gospel reading: Matthew 2:13-15, 19-23

Reflection

Has there been disagreement in any of our homes this Christmas? Has anyone in our family been jealous, unkind, intolerant, and perhaps even violent? Have some of us felt upset or rejected during the last few days? Many of us can answer 'Yes' to at least one of these questions.

This is very natural, given the stress of coping with extra people and visitors, and the additional work involved during this festive season, although it would not happen if everyone was celebrating the true meaning of Christmas. Emphasising the preparations and the trimmings of Christmas usually serves to undermine our understanding of the magnificent truth that God became human and lived among us, which is what we are invited to think about on this feast.

Ideally, then, we would not focus on family antagonisms or anything else that would disrupt our peace of mind and soul. But such human failings are one reason why we need the Feast of the Holy Family of Jesus, Mary and Joseph, because the feast provides an opportunity to reflect on our family lives.

We are reminded that the essence of good family and community life is respect. We are challenged to cherish and honour other family members. Experience teaches us that genuine family life exists only when everyone is sincere, compassionate, kind, humble, gentle, patient and forgiving.

These are the qualities that make family life pleasant and worthwhile. They ultimately derive from the authentic love that we have for God and one another. When family members live together in harmony, the home unquestionably provides the best environment for personal and communal faith development. Hence the home is often described as the domestic church.

At Christmas, families gather and exchange gifts. Christmas is meant to be a time of happiness and celebration. It ought to be a time of peace and goodwill. It would be wonderful if we could sustain this goodwill. Family life would thrive if everyone worked to make living together more enjoyable and refreshing.

Sadly, however, as Christmas and the Christmas holidays

end, many of us will be tired, frustrated and angry. Some will have feelings of regret. Others will have only memories of desertion and violence. Celebrating Christ's birth will have been meaningless.

However, it is not too late to change. We can try to be truly human together as we encourage and influence one another in the name of Jesus. For instance, there may be a member of our family with whom we could be more patient. We could make a start with this person, imitating the self-sacrificing love of Christ and the example of the saints, by being kind to that awkward relative. After all, great things are often achieved in small ways.

The same applies outside the boundaries of our human families. We, in the Church, are sisters and brothers in Jesus, and children of God our heavenly Father. Being members of God's family, we attempt to help and strengthen other people. Again, we can model ourselves on the Holy Family and try to live in harmony and peace.

Therefore, the Feast of the Holy Family reminds us that we are part of a human family and, equally, that we belong to God's family. In each case there are privileges and responsibilities. In our human families and in God's family, the Church, we work out our salvation together – as women, men and children living and working in love and peace. Let each one of us think of ways to make life more pleasant for other members in our family, and let us begin again today.

For meditation
Take the child and his mother with you, and escape into Egypt, and stay there until I tell you. (Mt 2:13)

Solemnity of Mary, Mother of God
Gospel reading: Luke 2:16-21

Reflection

In one sense, Mary was an ordinary person. She lived simply and humbly. Like most young Jewish women of her time, she was betrothed and, no doubt, looking forward to a happy life with her husband Joseph when the second part of the Jewish wedding ceremony was complete. Only then would they live together as husband and wife.

Prior to that, Jewish couples lived separately and their marriage was only consummated after the second part of the marriage ritual was completed. In the case of Mary and Joseph, the Church teaches that theirs was not a consummated marriage because Mary was a virgin, before, during and after the birth of her Son. Following the revelation to Joseph by an angel, he knew that Mary was specially chosen by God and that it was his role to guard and protect her and her child.

Mary was not interested in seeking people's attention. That is obvious from the gospels, where she constantly pointed people towards her Son. Yet she caught God's attention – if it is fair to make such a comment about God – because she was different from all other human beings, with the exception of her son Jesus.

The reason that she stood out in God's eyes was because, unlike other human beings, she never sinned. She succeeded in remaining completely faithful to his will. Therefore, although Mary was an ordinary person, in another sense she was quite extraordinary.

To say that Mary is the Mother of God does not imply that she is the Mother of the Trinity or the Mother of the Father or the Mother of the Holy Spirit. However, the Church teaches that Mary gave virginal birth to Jesus Christ, the Second Person of the Trinity who became human. Because God is one – Father and Son and Holy Spirit – we thus say that Mary is the Mother of God.

Perhaps, for some people, a more understandable title than Mother of God is *Theotokos* (Greek for God-bearer). This title was given to Mary in the second century, and formally proclaimed at the Council of Ephesus in 431AD, to indicate that she gave birth not just to a human being but to the Son of God himself. What is important, regardless of which title is preferred, is to acknowledge that Mary is indeed the Mother of God made human in Jesus our Lord and Saviour.

In honouring Mary as the Mother of God at the beginning of the New Year, we are not just remembering the debt we owe her for her selfless 'Yes' to God, but we are also recognising the divinity of Christ who is also truly human. It is necessary to do this because we can easily be tempted to assume that Jesus is merely human. The reality is that Jesus has two natures (divine and human) in one person.

In today's gospel reading, we are reminded that Mary 'treasured all these things and pondered them in her heart' (Lk 2:19), referring to all that had happened since the angel told her that if she accepted God's will for her – and she did have the option of refusing – she would become the Mother of the long-awaited Messiah, the Christ, who is God. We pray that we will treasure and ponder all that we have been taught to believe about the Mother of God and about who Jesus really is.

We are also reminded that, after visiting the newborn Jesus, the shepherds 'went back glorifying and praising God for all they had heard and seen; it was exactly as they had been told' (Lk 2:20). Let us, like the shepherds, glorify and praise God for the wonders he has done and for Mary the Mother of God.

For meditation
As for Mary, she treasured all these things and pondered them in her heart. (Lk 2:19)

Second Sunday after Christmas
Gospel reading: John 1:1-18

Reflection

During this earthly life, we will never be able to comprehend fully the mystery of Christmas. This is because God's ways are not our ways and our finite minds are unable to understand completely how God could become human while still remaining God. The idea of Jesus' two natures (divine and human) in one person does not make sense according to human logic.

One good reason why the Church, instead of quickly glossing over the feast of Christmas, asks us to reflect on its significance for at least eight days is the hope that the mystery of what has actually happened will impact on us and persuade us to change our lives radically. Otherwise, we would not be able to develop an appreciation of all that God has done for us so that we can attain salvation.

Today's gospel reading, which is commonly referred to as the prologue (that is, the introductory section) of John's Gospel, is the same gospel that was proclaimed during the Mass during the Day for the Feast of the Nativity. Thus we have another opportunity to reflect on that gospel's meaning and implications for Christian living. The essential message being communicated is that 'the Word was made flesh' and 'lived among us' (Jn 1:14). This is what is meant by the term Incarnation.

Incarnation literally means enfleshment. Specifically, according to the Christian revelation of God, it means that the Son of God, while remaining fully divine, became truly and fully human at a particular place and time in history. Of course, the Incarnation is not confined to the season of Christmas. It also includes the conception, suffering, death and resurrection of Jesus.

There are at least three phrases in the gospel reading that are especially challenging. First, we are reminded that 'the Word was the true light that enlightens all people; and he was coming into the world' (Jn 1:9). This teaches us that only in Jesus can we find the true light that is God. Every other light, such as John the Baptist, is a lesser light, a human being who can give us something of God's light. But by describing Jesus as the Word that was the true light, John the Evangelist is telling us that the Word of God – that is, God himself – is revealed in Jesus.

Secondly, we read that 'he [the Word] came to his own domain and his own people did not accept him. But to all who did accept him he gave power to become children of God' (Jn 1:11-12). God's grace is available to anyone who seeks the truth and not just the privileged Jewish race, God's Chosen People. This is true today since the Church of Christ is open to everyone. All repentant sinners and those seeking the truths revealed by God for our salvation can become members of the Church and thus be given the power to become children of God, as John's Gospel teaches.

Thirdly, we are told that 'no one has ever seen God; it is the only Son, who is nearest to the Father's heart, who has made him known' (Jn 1:18). This makes it clear that Jesus is the fullness of God's revelation.

The importance of Christmas is that we are reminded, annually, about the most momentous event in human history: the Incarnation. The fact that God became human and lived, worked, taught, worked miracles, suffered and died among us on this earth, is an event in history that can never be surpassed. We are invited, therefore, to be full of joy at Christmas, and to proclaim our faith in God's wonderful love.

The Incarnation occurred so that the crucifixion could take place – that we might gain salvation. That is why we celebrate and feast at Christmas. Without the Incarnation, there would not have been a salvific crucifixion. Our visits to the crib, therefore, always include a 'Thank you' to the infant Jesus for coming among us.

For meditation
The Word was made flesh, he lived among us. (Jn 1:14)

The Epiphany of the Lord
Gospel reading: Matthew 2:1-12

Reflection

The Feast of the Epiphany emphasises another dimension of the Christmas mystery. We remember that the Jewish people believed that, when God's promised Messiah would eventually arrive in their midst, he would set them free from tyranny and oppression, thereby inaugurating a new era of peace and justice. They understood themselves to be God's Chosen People and, as such, they were distinct from all other peoples.

That they were governed by the foreign Romans was an affront to this status as God's Chosen People and so the Jews looked forward eagerly to the coming of the promised Messiah, whom they wrongly believed would end the political interference of this foreign power in their national life.

Thus they misinterpreted the coming of the Messiah on two counts. First, they erroneously believed that the Messiah's mission was to free them from political tyranny when, in fact, God wanted to free them from the tyranny of sin. Secondly, they were mistaken to think that the promised Messiah was being sent only for their benefit.

The significance of the Magi (the wise men), who travelled from the east under the guidance of a star 'to do [the infant king of the Jews] homage' (Mt 2:2), is that the Messiah had come for everyone. They would have been categorised as gentiles by the Jews and the implication of their visit is that the Messiah was bringing the Good News that salvation is for all people of every time and place. Not that everyone will be saved – that is not the Church's teaching.

There is an important lesson here for us. None of us has an automatic right to be a member of the Church of Christ. That we have been granted the gift of faith is a reason for thanksgiving, but we must not think that we have a right to our Catholic faith. In the same way, we welcome others into the Church regardless of their social status or nationality. We are all sinners and, as long as we repent, we are welcome at the altar of God. No political affiliations or national or racial issues have any place in our attitude to other Catholics.

That is in essence the message of Christmas: salvation has come and is for all people, not just the few. The opening prayer of today's Mass summarises the message of the Epiphany: Let us pray that we will be guided by the light of faith. Father, you revealed your Son to the nations by the guidance of a star. Lead us to your glory in heaven by the light of faith.

Perhaps we could adopt the attitude of the Magi. In the gospel we learn that 'the sight of the star filled them with delight' and that, having found the child and 'falling to their knees they did him homage' and 'offered him gifts of gold, frankincense and myrrh' (Mt 2:10-11). So we offer him our gifts and talents for the service of the building up of his kingdom here on earth.

Then, too, we welcome the revelation about God and his commandments, which is offered to us by the Church. We embrace its teaching which is always pointing us in the direction of Christ if we are to live in imitation of the Magi. Likewise, we imitate the example of the Magi by falling to our knees and paying Christ homage. When the Magi realised who this child was, the first thing they did was to fall to their knees in adoration. This is a central lesson of Christmas and we resolve to practice it without delay.

For meditation
We saw his star as it rose and have come to do the king homage. (Mt 2:2)

The Baptism of the Lord
Gospel reading: Matthew 3:13-17

Reflection

Liturgical time is cyclical and passes rather quickly. It must do so because, every year, it remembers and makes effective the entire story of God's salvation of his people ('the gradual unfolding of the drama of salvation history', as scholars often depict it).

We recently commemorated the birth of our Saviour on the first Christmas, as we do every Christmas. During those days we celebrated the reality of the Word becoming flesh, of God becoming human (the Incarnation), when we reflected on the newborn infant Jesus wrapped in swaddling clothes and lying in a manger.

Now, however, within a few days we have moved rapidly to Jesus' public life, by-passing his adolescent and early adult years, which could be described as the hidden years – although the gospel records that he lived under the authority of Mary and Joseph in Nazareth. Today we commemorate his baptism in the River Jordan when the Holy Spirit descended on him at the beginning of his public ministry.

Baptism was given a new meaning by Jesus and all Christians share in that meaning. We have been baptised into the Christian faith by water and the Holy Spirit, and our Christian faith teaches us that sacramental baptism is the gateway to the other sacraments.

There is powerful symbolism associated with water. It can sustain life and cleanse, by its thirst-quenching and purifying qualities. But it can also destroy that same life through drowning. Thus water has the potential to give life and to cause death. Too much water is as damaging as too little water.

The religious symbolism of water in sacramental baptism revolves around our dying to alienation from God through the washing away of our sins, and around our new identity which is nourished and deepened by our sharing in God's life and by being incorporated into the Body of Christ which is the Church.

That is why we say that, in baptism, we die with Christ, going into the tomb with him, and we rise with him to a new and everlasting life. The significance of God's invitation to share in this newness of life offered in baptism is well summarised in the words: 'This is my Son, the Beloved; my favour rests on him' (Mt 3:17).

Baptism is powerfully effective in our lives. The sacrament does what it is a sign of – in other words, it is efficacious. Thus it washes away Original Sin and restores us to the life of grace, which is God's life in the soul. This baptismal dignity will continue to lead us to God if, when we sin, we repent and avail of the sacrament of reconciliation.

Throughout our lives, if we open our hearts to God's loving presence and if we listen to the word of God, then our souls will be nourished and live in a healthy state of union with God's will.

As we celebrate the Feast of the Baptism of the Lord, we have a timely liturgical reminder that we have been baptised into Christ's death and resurrection. We share in his risen life through baptism and we know that God has made an irreversible commitment to us.

Let us renew again our commitment to the baptised life and its meaning which, from our perspective, focuses on living in faithfulness to the teaching of Christ and his Church regardless of the difficulties and challenges of that teaching. Let us recognise once more our need of God's saving help in our everyday lives and let us rejoice that our souls will live because of the eternal life brought through the water of baptism at the outset of our Christian life.

For meditation
As soon as Jesus was baptised he came up from the water, and suddenly the heavens opened and he saw the Spirit of God descending like a dove and coming down on him. (Mt 3:16)

The Season of Lent

First Sunday of Lent
Gospel reading: Matthew 4:1-11

Reflection

Being Christians, we are part of the covenant people. We belong to the people whom God has chosen as his own people and with whom he established a covenant relationship.

A covenant is an agreement between two or more parties. It is an alliance or partnership between them and it involves a commitment from each of the participating parties to be faithful to the agreement that they made when beginning their special relationship. In the Old Testament, the Chosen People were the Jews.

Later, Jesus – himself a Jew – developed the covenant relationship by establishing a new means of conducting our relationship with God through the Church which, according to the paragraph 877 of the *Catechism of the Catholic Church*, is 'the new Israel'.

Therefore, as people in the covenant relationship with God, we are unique. Not only in the sense of being privileged due to our membership of the Church, but also in the sense of having serious obligations. In that relationship, God promises to be our God and we, in turn, promise to be his people. These promises are binding forever and faithfulness is necessary.

The covenant relationship requires obedience from us. In return, God will reward us with great graces and, ultimately, with heaven. There is an example of this in the account of Jesus being led by the Spirit into the wilderness to be tempted by the devil (see Mt 4:1-11). Even after fasting for forty days, Jesus resisted the devil's temptations and succeeded in sending him away. By remaining faithful to his Father's will, Jesus taught that if we resist temptation we will not become slaves to sin.

As with Jesus during his temptations in the wilderness, God the Father has never been, and could not be, unfaithful to his promise to be our God at all times and in all places. God does not change and his promise is irrevocable. Throughout human history, however, God's chosen people were often unfaithful to the covenant and it has needed renewal by them. Thus the covenant relationship was always cyclical with repeating cycles of fidelity, sin, punishment and reconciliation.

In the Hebrew scriptures we read that the covenant was renewed several times after the people had been disloyal and had abandoned living in accordance with God's commandments. The renewal was expressed in various signs and rituals. For example, the sign of the covenant that God made with Noah was the rainbow. Similarly, the sign of the covenant that God made with Abraham (that his descendants would be as many as the stars) was male circumcision. The sign of the covenant that God made with Moses on Mount Sinai was the Ten Commandments.

Subsequently, in the New Testament we read that the new and eternal covenant between God and his Chosen People was sealed by the blood of Christ in his suffering and death. The sign of this covenant is ritualised in the sacrament of baptism. In baptism we die with Christ and rise to new life with him. Living the baptised life authentically, as evidenced by our faithfulness to God's commandments, is the proof that we are taking the covenant seriously. Central to the covenant relationship is a continual turning towards God and turning away from sin, which is what damages and breaks the covenant.

During Lent, through prayer, fasting and charitable works, we renew our covenant relationship with God. We are called to undergo conversion through repentance for our sins so that we will be ready to appreciate the meaning of the death and resurrection of Christ at Easter. The ritual sign of renewing our baptismal commitment is celebrating the sacrament of reconciliation. Lent is a particularly appropriate time for us to go to confession and, in the spirit of true repentance, to be assured that our sins are forgiven.

The message of Lent is summarised in the words spoken to us on Ash Wednesday when the sign of the cross is traced on our foreheads with the blessed ashes: Turn away from sin and be faithful to the gospel. Now is the time to begin the process of conversion so that our commitment to God may become as unbreakable as his commitment to us.

For meditation
Jesus was led by the Spirit out into the wilderness to be tempted by the devil. (Mt 4:1)

Second Sunday of Lent
Gospel reading: Matthew 17:1-9

Reflection

During Lent, while we prepare to commemorate the death and resurrection of Christ and celebrate the everlasting life he shares with us at Easter, we are invited to review our lives in the context of our Christian faith and the teachings of his Church. Also, we are encouraged to repent of our sins and to do penance for them so that we can renew our relationship with Christ. Hence Lent is characterised by prayer, fasting and penance.

But these penitential aspects of Lent are not intended to discourage us even if they challenge us severely. Indeed, the example of the Church's saints teaches us that those who are most disciplined and faithful to Christ are those who display the greatest joy. It is a mistake to connect penance with unhappiness. The opposite is true. In fact, our society is full of people who are pursuing hedonistic pleasure, which they mistake for happiness, and who are miserable in the pursuit of false happiness.

Lent is meant to be fundamentally a good experience because the established Lenten practices facilitate our ongoing conversion to the Gospel. So our prayer during Lent needs to be enthusiastically similar to the words spoken by Peter to Jesus during the Transfiguration: 'Lord, it is wonderful for us to be here' (Mt 17:4).

Lent offers us a yearly opportunity to undergo conversion from sin. It is only when we abandon sin that we can truly begin the pursuit of authentic happiness and experience the joy of the saints in our lives. Sin alienates us from God and, often, from other people. So it is imperative that we eradicate it from our lives.

Then we are drawn closer to Jesus and that is our purpose here on earth – to become close to Jesus because God made us to know, love and serve him in this world so that we may be happy with him forever in heaven. An appropriate prayer, therefore, is: It is wonderful for us to be here.

However, as we know, Lent is quite demanding and requires considerable spiritual discipline, especially if we are not in the habit of fasting and doing penance. It would be impossible for us to embrace wholeheartedly the challenges of the Gospel while depending on our own resolve alone. For that reason, we need to remember Jesus' consoling words to his close friends when they were frightened on the mountain: 'Stand up, do not be afraid' (Mt 17:7). We are never alone.

Our Lenten motto becomes: It is wonderful for us to be here. In addition, we are encouraged by Jesus' words: 'Do not be afraid.' They remind us that he is in control. Jesus also spoke these words to Peter in the boat when a storm raged all around them. He was teaching them – and us – not to fret but to trust in God's providence.

A central message of Lent is that, at least metaphorically, we put on sackcloth and ashes, do penance for our sins and seek to make progress in the spiritual life, thereby uniting ourselves with the suffering Christ. By taking such practical steps, we can be sure of pleasing God and growing in true happiness and real joy.

For meditation
Jesus took with him Peter and James and his brother John and led them up a high mountain where they could be alone. (Mt 17:1)

Third Sunday of Lent

Gospel reading: John 4:5-42

Reflection

From whom or from where do we draw life? This question can be answered on several levels. Maybe we draw life from our spouses as we experience their love. Perhaps we draw life from our children whenever we rejoice in their talents and achievements. We may draw life from the fulfilment and satisfaction provided by our work that makes a real difference to the quality of life for us and for other people. Or we may draw life from our hobbies that renew our enthusiasm for life.

However, on a deeper level – that of the depths of our being – from whom do we draw life? For Christians, there is only one completely satisfactory answer to this question. Christians believe that God is the sole author of life and that they draw life in all its fullness from God, in and through his Son Jesus Christ. The fountain of living water is to be found with Jesus: a fountain from which eternal life gushes.

We all share in the fruits of this living water because, through baptism, we share in the death and resurrection of Christ. We have become his brothers and sisters and, together in the Church, we are God's family on this earth nourished by the real presence of Christ in the Eucharist. During Lent, even as we fast and do penance, we are challenged to rediscover the person of Jesus from whom we draw life, the only life that ultimately matters.

Therefore, we need to pray to God asking that Jesus, the living water, may strengthen us in our weaknesses. If only we could drink once again with pure hearts from the fountain of life, hearts that have been renewed by a true spirit of repentance and reconciliation. When we respond to the loving presence of the God in our lives, we learn to love and respect other people.

Like most people, the Samaritan woman whom Jesus met at the well was seeking life and the truth. Yet she was unknowingly speaking to the Life and the Truth. Jesus offered to make a real difference in her life while she listened attentively to his words. We can make a real difference to others and ourselves by listening attentively to the word of God, the true fountain of life, and by living according to its message of hope and life.

Therefore, let our prayer for today and always be: God our Father, we draw our life from you. You are the fountain of life. Your word is living water without which we die. Enable us, through the death and resurrection of your Son and through the inspiration of your Holy Spirit, to grow in love and understanding. Accompany us on our journey through life, so that we may go with confidence into your world as a new creation – one body drawing life from the one fountain of life – so that the world may believe.

For meditation
But anyone who drinks the water that I will give will never be thirsty again: the water that I shall give will turn into a spring inside him, welling up to eternal life. (Jn 4:14)

Fourth Sunday of Lent
Gospel reading: John 9:1-41

Reflection

One of my friends was born blind. Consequently, he is unable to marvel at the colours of the rainbow. He is incapable of appreciating the subtle differences between the various shades of green in the garden shrubs and trees. He cannot enjoy the beauty of the stained glass windows in his local church as the sunlight shines through them. In short, he cannot see the beauty of God's creation.

However, my blind friend's other senses – hearing, speech, touch and smell – are exceptionally alert and they help him to compensate for his blindness by enabling him to experience and appreciate his surroundings in different ways. Yet he seems to be disadvantaged when compared to most other people because, unlike them, he cannot see with his eyes. He lives in a world of darkness and during this life he will never truly understand what it is to see and to be guided by light.

Thankfully, although physically blind, my friend has learned to 'see' in other ways. He believes in God and, for him as it must be for all of us, believing is seeing. It is often said that 'seeing is believing'. Nevertheless, it is faith that brings true sight and, from the perspective of faith, 'believing is seeing'. My friend has seen God in many areas of his life without depending on his eyes and, having experienced God's love, he believes in God's goodness and providential care. True sight, then, is really insight.

Sadly, there has always been physical blindness in our world. But physical blindness is not the only type of blindness that affects people, nor is it the most damaging. A far more harmful blindness is the spiritual blindness that results from sin. This spiritual blindness is evident in the lives of people who are confused or lost, often having no moral guidance.

Unlike physical blindness, spiritual blindness occurs when people either refuse or are unable to accept Jesus Christ as the Way, the Truth and the Life. The well known proverb is appropriate: 'There is none so blind as those who will not see!' Here, the phrase 'those who will not' means 'those who do not wish to' or 'those who refuse to'.

Unfortunately, many of us are spiritually blind without realising it. We need to learn that in recognising our personal sinfulness our spiritual blindness begins to be healed. Jesus brings healing from sin into our lives through his Church and the sacraments, especially the sacrament of reconciliation. When we celebrate this sacrament with the proper disposition we meet the risen Lord who heals us and gives us life. Believing is seeing.

Although my friend lives in constant darkness, he has many opportunities to see as a result of his faith. Ironically, many of us who can see clearly with our eyes are increasingly blind to God's presence around us because of our lack of faith and our sin. We are being challenged to invite Jesus to heal our spiritual blindness so that we may share his insight. Then our witness to the Good News will lead us to dispel the spiritual darkness in our world. God has chosen each one of us to reveal his love to the world. First of all, however, we need to believe in God so that, like my friend who is blind, believing we may see.

For meditation
The blind man went off and washed himself, and came away with his sight restored. (Jn 9:7)

Fifth Sunday of Lent
Gospel reading: John 11:1-45

Reflection

How much is our faith like Martha's faith? During Jesus' visit to Martha and Mary after the death of Lazarus, Martha professed true faith in him. When Jesus asked her if she believed that he was the Resurrection and the Life, she acknowledged him as 'the Christ, the Son of God, the one who was to come into this world' (Jn 11:27). Martha was one of the few people in the New Testament who expressed such a faith in Jesus before his own death and resurrection. Another person who expressed a similar faith was Peter (see Mt 16:16). Thus Martha's faith anticipated a truly Easter faith.

Martha believed that physical death was not the end. Instead, physical death gave way to eternal life because, for her, Jesus Christ was (and is) the Lord of life. Martha looked forward to the resurrection of the body on the last day. Meanwhile she maintained a sure and certain hope that is characteristic of the basic Christian hope which is at the heart of our Christian faith.

At Easter, we celebrate Jesus' resurrection from the dead. Because he is risen, all of us will likewise be raised from the dead. We are all invited to share in his death and resurrection and, provided we are committed to the newness of the risen life that he offers us, we gain an everlasting place in heaven. This means that if we turn away from the sins that separate us from God – for example, irreligion, theft, adultery, disregard for parents, and drunkenness – we will gain heaven for eternity. This is the real meaning of Easter, and the resurrection of Jesus from the dead is at the centre of our Christian faith.

Therefore, as Paul teaches (see 1 Cor 15:14), if Jesus is not raised from the dead, then our faith is in vain and we are foolish people. The resurrection of Jesus from the dead is the proof that everything he said and did in his public ministry is true, bearing in mind that what he is portrayed as saying and doing in the gospel has been painted with 'resurrection spectacles'. Sharing in his risen life demands that we remain faithful to his teaching and committed to his Church.

The all-important question for us at Eastertide is: Do we sincerely believe, like Martha, that Jesus Christ is the Resurrection and the Life? In other words, do we accept that he is raised from the dead and that he is the Lord of life? How can we have the sure and certain hope that was characteristic of her faith? Martha provides an inspiring example of Easter faith. Despite her obvious grief at the death of Lazarus, she put her faith completely in Christ. We are challenged to do the same.

How much is our faith like Martha's faith? Let our prayer today be: Lord, our God, strengthen our faith in Jesus Christ, the Resurrection and the Life. May we learn from Martha's example so that the message of Easter may change our lives and lead us to eternal life.

For meditation

I am the resurrection. If anyone believes in me, even though he dies he will live, and whoever lives and believes in me will never die. (Jn 11:25-26)

Passion Sunday (Palm Sunday)

Gospel reading (The Procession): Matthew 21:1-11
Gospel reading (The Mass): Matthew 26:14 – 27:66

Reflection

The long gospel reading (including the gospel preceding the entrance procession) in the Palm Sunday liturgy provides us with an introduction to the scandalous events of Holy Week. These events range from the people's adulation of Jesus to their demands that he suffer a humiliating and shameful death at the hands of the Romans. Palm Sunday and Holy Week present us with bewildering contradictions in how the people treated Jesus.

At first, the people treated him like a king. There was tremendous joy and excitement among them when he entered Jerusalem – triumphantly in their estimation. They greeted him as the Messiah. In John's Gospel, the crowd is portrayed as having heard Jesus refer to himself as the 'Resurrection and the Life' and they knew that he was 'the one who is to come'.

Less than one week later, however, the crowd, according to Matthew's Gospel, insisted that Jesus be crucified. Their attitude towards him had changed fundamentally and irrevocably. We might well ask: Why? The reason was that he had challenged them to change their lifestyles in imitation of his example, although some scholars suggest that the basis for Jesus' death was his actions in the Temple which had infuriated them. In any event, what a fickle and unreliable people!

Many of us today would not admit to being fickle or to having a superficial faith. We claim to be very different from those people who demanded Jesus' death because we think that we would have behaved differently towards him. However, we forget that it was our sins and the sins of all people that Jesus took on himself when he was crucified.

Therefore, each one of us is partially culpable for Jesus' betrayal and death. We cannot blame his Jewish contemporaries for the scandal of his death. We too are God's beloved people. Yet we have betrayed God's love when we have sinned.

In contrast to us, God is loyal, steadfast and completely dependable. Fortunately God's love for us is not dependant on our positive response to him. God's love for us in Christ is unfaltering. Jesus died 'for our sins' (1 Cor 15:3). In doing so, he emptied himself totally for our sake, and for the sake of all people of every time and place – although his self-emptying also includes the Incarnation (see Phil 2). Thus he brought us life on the cross even though he lost his own life there. In the face of human betrayal he proved that God's love for us is endless.

The crucial questions for us during Holy Week are: How do we treat Jesus? In what ways do we praise him and welcome him when we meet him in our churches and as we celebrate the sacraments? Sometimes we betray him as we quickly return to our sinful ways. As we accompany him on his final journey to Jerusalem, will we stay with him or will we abandon him like many other people? Can we accept the challenge to become repentant or will we avoid the discomfort of God's will leading us where God wants us to be instead of where we want to be?

There are so many questions. But, then, Holy Week is *the* week for questions in the lives of Christians everywhere.

For meditation
My Father, if it possible, let this cup pass from me. Nevertheless, let it be as you, not I, would have it. (Jn 26:39)

The Season of Easter

Easter Sunday

Gospel reading (Mass of Easter Night): Matthew 28:1-10
Gospel reading (Mass of the Day): John 20:1-9

Reflection

The resurrection of Jesus from the dead was a clear wake-up call to his disciples and all the other people who had 'failed to understand the teaching of scripture, that he must rise from the dead' (Jn 20:9). His resurrection challenged them to wake from the sleep of their disbelief and indifference. By going into hiding and even denying all knowledge of Jesus when he was arrested, they had obviously missed the central message of his preaching and teaching.

But when the reality of Jesus' rising from the dead impacted on them, they began to understand that it was quite consistent with all that he had said and done before his death on the cross. So they must have asked themselves why they had not listened to him and recognised him for who he is: the Son of God and the Saviour of the world. As they thought back on the sayings, parables and miracles of Jesus' ministry, they gradually understood the truth of his claim to be 'the Way, the Truth and the Life' (Jn 14:6).

The realisation that the risen Lord was in their midst changed their lives radically. His several post-resurrection appearances gave them a renewed sense of hope and they became witnesses to his teaching.

The same joy and enthusiasm are meant to apply to us. However, there is also an important difference. Unlike the first disciples, we have the advantage of two millennia of Christian tradition and reflection. We have many opportunities for faith formation that did not exist in the early Church. Yet, even with the benefit of hindsight, we are equally or sometimes even more hesitant than the first-century disciples to make the necessary leap of faith in Jesus who is risen from the dead.

The significance of what happened at Easter is well summarised in the first Preface of Easter which states that 'by dying he [Jesus] destroyed our death; by rising he restored our life'.

This was what Simon Peter and John realised when they arrived at the empty tomb. Effectively, they saw and they believed.

In contrast, we did not see the empty tomb. So our Christian faith invites us to reverse the order by believing first and then, through our belief, seeing. Saint Thomas Aquinas taught that this is real faith: not to go looking for the evidence and then, when we satisfy ourselves that the necessary proof exists, to embrace the faith. Instead, it is the other way round: embracing God in faith and then seeking to deepen our knowledge and understanding.

Our belief in the risen Lord originates in the witness of those who accompanied him. We journey with him, but in a different way from those who met him and walked with him and ate with him and touched him after his resurrection from the dead. Jesus' resurrection from the dead is the definitive proof that physical death is not the end. There is life after death. And God invites all of us to use this earthly life to prepare for the next life.

With renewed faith and hope this day, let the words of the opening prayer for the Mass of Easter Sunday become our prayer: Let us pray that the risen Christ will raise us up and renew our lives. God our Father, by raising Christ your Son you conquered the power of death and opened for us the way to eternal life. Let our celebration today raise us up and renew our lives by the Spirit that is within us.

For meditation
Till this moment they had failed to understand the teaching of scripture, that he must rise from the dead. (Jn 20:9)

Second Sunday of Easter
Gospel reading: John 20:19-31

Reflection

When we celebrate the sacrament of reconciliation, we are assured that our sins are forgiven and that we will have God's help to avoid sin in the future.

What is a sacrament? A sacrament is an outward sign of an inward grace. There are seven such sacraments in the Catholic Church. However, the seven sacraments are not simply signs like other signs in our lives. Unlike other signs and symbols, the sacraments are signs or symbols that bring about in our lives what they signify.

For example, although we might say that a washing machine is a symbol of cleanliness, we know that it is much more than that because it actually does what it symbolises: it cleans. In the same way a sacrament signifies an actual meeting – a personal encounter – with the risen Lord Jesus. Thus the sacrament of reconciliation is not just a sign or symbol of God's forgiveness. Through it, we are truly absolved from our sins. The sacrament does what it signifies.

In celebrating the sacrament of reconciliation, what, we may ask, is the inward grace being celebrated? It is the process of the inner change that is happening because of conversion away from the darkness of sin towards the radiant light of Christ. But this inner change is not outwardly recognisable, precisely because it is interior to the penitent's life. Therefore, there needs to be some outward sign that, in some way, manifests the inner change that is occurring.

For the sacrament to be celebrated properly, the penitent first confesses his/her sins. The naming of the sins in the presence of the priest indicates that the penitent is accepting personal responsibility for them.

Secondly, the penitent expresses genuine sorrow for the sins by praying the act of contrition. Again, the vocalising of this prayer is a sign of the penitent's sorrow and desire for conversion.

Thirdly, and crucially, the priest speaks the words of absolution that, because of the grace of ordination, mediate God's forgiveness. As the penitent listens to the words of absolution and sees the priest make the sign of the cross, the penitent realises that his/her sins are forgiven.

Fourthly, and finally, the penitent performs the penance given by the priest. The penance is another outward sign of the inward grace. The penance in itself does not undo the harm caused by the sins but is simply a gesture on the penitent's part that the process of interior conversion is progressing. Nonetheless, the penance is an important activity that demonstrates outwardly what is happening inwardly in the penitent's life.

We all need to experience reconciliation in our lives. The sacrament of reconciliation enables us to experience God's forgiveness for our sins. Through the outward signs of confessing sins, praying the act of contrition, receiving absolution and doing the penance, we demonstrate our interior conversion and we complete the process of sacramental reconciliation.

For meditation
Receive the Holy Spirit. For those whose sins you forgive, they are forgiven; for those whose sins you retain, they are retained. (Jn 20:22-23)

Third Sunday of Easter
Gospel reading: Luke 24:13-35

Reflection
The story about the two disciples meeting Jesus on the road to Emmaus and how they recognised him at 'the breaking of the bread' (Lk 24:35) teaches us much about the Eucharist and, in particular, the way in which it provides food for eternal life.

Food satisfies our physical hunger. However, sharing a meal also satisfies a greater hunger, the hunger for the deeper human need of companionship. Sharing a meal facilitates interpersonal exchange and, in so doing, promotes important human values. It symbolises and brings about unity among people.

Similarly, the Eucharist provides food and deeper nourishment for our spiritual lives because it is the Bread of Life. Throughout the gospels we read that Jesus enjoyed gatherings and meals. He often sought companionship with other people, that resulted in him sharing something of himself and, ultimately, at the Last Supper, all of himself, with them. He used such occasions to teach the truth about himself.

The love and generosity of Jesus in responding to the confusion and hopelessness of the two disciples on the road to Emmaus, and his teaching them the fuller meaning of his actions, offer us an insight into his own total self-giving for others at the Last Supper and in his suffering and death.

Jesus wants his followers to imitate his example. The challenging question for all of us who are Jesus' disciples is: Do we live in memory of him when we gather to share the Eucharist? In other words, how do we remember all that he said and in what ways do we practise what he did? Just as Jesus gave his life for the life of the world, so we are being challenged to follow his example, while acknowledging that it can be extremely difficult to put the interests of other people before our own.

Therefore, the challenge of celebrating the Eucharist is: Can we respond to people as Jesus did? In effect, can we, in and through our own convictions and lifestyles that are nourished by the Body and Blood, Soul and Divinity, of Christ received when we celebrate the Eucharist, join with him in satisfying the spiritual hunger in other people's lives? If we can, then we are living Eucharistic lives that flow from the selfless and self-giving life of Jesus Christ.

Meal times often degenerate into a hastily-eaten snack or a quick take-away. Similarly, the celebration of the Eucharist can become just another hastily-observed obligation or a meaningless ritual. But the Mass is much more than a meal.

So let us try to make meal times at home and our participation in the Eucharist a time of genuine sharing and enrichment. In doing so, we acknowledge our gratitude for Christ's abiding presence and nourishment in the form of bread and wine that have become his Body and Blood providing us with food for eternal life.

For meditation
And their eyes were opened and they recognised him; but he had vanished from their sight. (Lk 24:31)

Fourth Sunday of Easter
Gospel reading: John 10:1-10

Reflection

There are several reasons for the lack of interest in priesthood as a way of life. Among them is undoubtedly the model of priesthood that is currently practised. Obligatory celibacy is another reason. But the most serious reason is the growing secularisation of society and the consequent absence of faith from the lives of many people.

In general, society has become more overtly materialistic and individualistic. Attentiveness to sacred and religious matters has waned. The Church is perceived to be a remnant from the past that has little or no relevance now. In such a situation, the significance of priesthood becomes meaningless. So it is not surprising that fewer men seriously consider being a priest.

A priest is a man who, having already been baptised, receives the sacrament of holy orders when the bishop ordains him. The priest is ordained to serve as a spiritual leader of God's people in the local church. He imitates Jesus the Good Shepherd. This means that his essential role is to form and support a Christian community based on the proclamation of God's word and the celebration of the sacraments. In particular, the priest presides at formal gatherings for worship, especially the celebration of the Eucharist. Thus he facilitates people in the expression and nurturing of their relationships with God.

What, then, distinguishes the ordained (or ministerial) priest from the priesthood of other members of the Church? The essential nature of ordained priesthood that distinguishes it from baptism is that the ordained priest acts 'in the person of Christ' (in Latin: *in persona Christi*) or stands in the place of Christ, especially when he presides at the celebration of the Mass and when he absolves sin. This is not to deny Christ's presence in the people assembled.

Crucially, ordination to the priesthood brings about a change in the character of the man being ordained. This means that the priest, whose person is conformed or moulded to Christ, becomes 'another Christ' (in Latin: *alter Christus*). The priest is called to imitate the Good Shepherd who lays down his life for his flock. Thhe priest is charged with the task of knowing, loving and caring for those who have been entrusted to his pastoral care.

Being a priest can sometimes be difficult. This is not to suggest that other vocations, for example, to married life or to religious life, have no problems. They most certainly do. The life of a priest requires faith, permanent commitment, prayer and humility. It is about self-sacrifice and total service of God and his people. But it is also a rewarding and fulfilling way of life.

Priests share in and help to make sense of the joyful and sad occasions in people's lives. They regularly have opportunities to share Christ's healing and life-giving power with people so that life can be more meaningful. They teach people to be faithful to the Good News so that they are like sheep who follow Jesus the Lord who is the Good Shepherd.

No priest is perfect. Like all people, priests are always being called to conversion. We live in a society where confusion abounds and in a Church where many members are disillusioned. We need priests today more than ever because our world is crying out for signs of hope and God's presence in many situations that have become distressing and futile.

There is still much work to be done in building the kingdom of God in our world. Priests are absolutely necessary for this task. It is time for us to pray more fervently for the priests that we have and for more vocations to the ordained priesthood. It may even be time for some of us to consider pursuing the priestly vocation or, perhaps, re-imaging the model of priesthood.

For meditation
I have come so that they may have life and have it to the full. (Jn 10:10)

Fifth Sunday of Easter
Gospel reading: John 14:1-12

Reflection

Jesus is the Way, the Truth and the Life. If we cannot believe this, then Jesus joins a long list of influential religious leaders who have tried to make a difference to the world throughout human history. He remains one of many leaders, all of whom may be legitimate and relevant but none of whom is unique and absolutely necessary for salvation. Accordingly, neither is the Church necessary for salvation because one religion is as good as another.

However, if we are convinced that Jesus is the Way, the Truth and the Life – as he taught in his preaching – we believe that he is divine as well as human and we accept the uniqueness of his saving death and resurrection. Furthermore, we acknowledge the uniqueness of Christianity among the various world religions and we recognise the absolute necessity of the Church for salvation. The Church is necessary because the Church is the Body of Christ, and Jesus Christ is the Way, the Truth and the Life.

What does it mean, then, to claim that Jesus is the Way, the Truth and the Life? Very simply, it means that Jesus is *the* way to our true home in heaven. He is the only way because he teaches the truth and because the Father's life is in him. So the fullness of God's revelation is found in Jesus. All of what God wishes us to know about his nature and his will is to be glimpsed in Jesus who manifests God's unconditional love and forgiveness. He dies for us and for all other sinners so that we may have eternal life.

God is to be found in Jesus who is Christ the Lord. That is why Jesus told his disciples that, 'to have seen me is to have seen the Father' (Jn 14:9). Jesus came into the world to teach us about God. When we accept Jesus as our Lord and Saviour, we are assured that we are in direct, personal contact with God.

But Jesus is not the Way, the Truth and Life just for those who know him and believe in him explicitly. He is also the Way, the Truth and the Life for all people who are saved, for all people who gain an everlasting dwelling place in heaven. Christians believe and teach that Jesus Christ is the sole mediator between God and all people. Salvation for everyone is achieved only through the merits of his death on the cross, although people from other religions and none do not accept this.

Jesus is the Universal Saviour. His life and ministry teach us all we need to know about God. His death wins eternal life for us. His resurrection from the dead gives us hope in this life and in life after death. He leads us to God, our heavenly Father. That is why we believe that he is the Way, the Truth and the Life.

For meditation
Do not let your hearts be troubled. Trust in God still, and trust in me. (Jn 14:1)

Sixth Sunday of Easter
Gospel reading: John 14:15-21

Reflection

We do not instinctively associate the concept of love with the demand to be faithful to a series of rules. People often speak about love as if it is in opposition to rules and regulations: 'all you need is love' and 'love and do what you will' are the type of sayings that are used in discussions as evidence that we do not need to worry about rules.

Yet, in the farewell speech to his disciples, Jesus was uncompromising when he explained the necessary connection between loving him and keeping his commandments: 'If you love me you will keep my commandments' (Jn 14:15).

In that speech, Jesus dealt with several other concerns. But he then returned to the link between love and the commandments: 'Anyone who receives my commandments and keeps them will be one who loves me; and anybody who loves me will be loved by my Father, and I shall love him and show myself to him' (Jn 14:21).

The central commandment of Jesus' teaching was to love God and love neighbour. That commandment summarised the basic moral behaviours and ritual practices that Jesus required from his disciples. Those behaviours and practices formed the charter of what it meant for them to live as his followers.

Jesus' moral teaching is best summarised in the Sermon on the Mount (see Mt 5-7) or the Sermon on the Plain (see Lk 6) where he expands the Ten Commandments, making them more demanding. For example, the commandment not to kill is developed to prohibit undue anger with another person, and the commandment not to commit adultery is developed to prohibit even lustful thinking.

The ethical teaching of Jesus provides us with definite instructions for everyday living. It stresses the need for correct and respectful relationships with God and with one another. It teaches us that we cannot separate our relationship with God from our various relationships with other people. This means that we cannot have a straightforward vertical relationship with God without also having a horizontal relationship with God through our relationships with the people we meet in everyday life.

The fundamental message of Jesus' moral teaching is that we are obligated to love God and our neighbour. We cannot love one without the other. It is impossible to compartmentalise God and people such that they remain unconnected. Our dealings with others have implications for our friendship with God. This is how, in practice, we connect love and rules. If we love God, we will keep his commandments. If we love our neighbour, we will not treat him/her unjustly.

Nowadays, many people dismiss moral imperatives as being irrelevant to modern life. They are often viewed negatively because they are judged to be imposing limitations on our freedom. However, that is not so. Fidelity to Jesus' commandments enables us to live freely in the presence of God who cares for us. Contrary to popular opinion, the purpose of Jesus' moral demands is to enable us to appreciate the freedom of living according to God's will. It is not to make our lives miserable. Faithfulness to his commandments is the benchmark of our love for him and, in fact, for ourselves and our neighbour.

The teaching of Jesus offers us clear instructions to enable us to be to be faithful to God's will. It summarises what is required in order to live a wholesome life that reflects God's truth and beauty. Its purpose is to rid our lives of selfishness and self-centredness so that we can learn to put God and other people first, and ourselves last.

When our consciences are formed by Jesus' teaching, we know the difference between right and wrong. Living according to his teaching ensures genuine happiness in this life and eternal happiness in heaven.

For meditation
If you love me you will keep my commandments. (Jn14:15)

The Ascension of the Lord
Gospel reading: Matthew 28:16-20

Reflection

We are familiar with the frequently used saying 'to come full circle', which means that people or things, having set out on a journey or task, have returned to where they started. They have success-fully completed the cycle and are back at the beginning. This applies particularly to our thoughts about Jesus on the Feast of the Ascension.

In one sense, the Ascension celebrates that Jesus has come full circle because, having come from the Father to accomplish a specific mission, he returns to the Father having achieved what he was sent to do. And he was sent to save us from spiritual death and alienation from God that is due to our sins.

But in another sense, the Ascension marks the passing on of the baton by Jesus to his apostles. At the beginning of his public ministry, he had preached that the kingdom of heaven was close and he had challenged people to repent of their sins and believe in the Good News, which involves putting the teachings of Christ into practice in their lives. Now the responsibility for that ministry was being passed on to the apostles and disciples. They were mandated to continue his saving work, drawing all nations to the truth of the Gospel.

Jesus' departure from the earth and his return to heaven did not mean that his apostles and disciples would remain alone in their mission. Although he would no longer be physically pre-sent, he told them: 'And know that I am with you always; yes, to the end of time' (Mt 28:20). So there was no need for them to worry or to be lacking in confidence because he would be spirit-ually present, especially in the sacramental life of the Church.

He also promised to send the Holy Spirit who would guide them in their various activities. In fact, the Church will never be alone and it will never be abandoned by the risen Lord Jesus. We celebrate that reality today as we mark the close of the post-resurrection appearances of Jesus – apart from his appearance during the conversion of Saul (see Acts 9:3-7).

The message of the Ascension is clear. The saving work of Christ is now being handed over to the Church. The baton is

being passed on to us. Just as in a relay race, it is imperative that
we do not drop the baton. In other words, the responsibility for
passing on the faith rests with us. Let us carry the faith with
courage and conviction and let us pass it on to those we meet.

We remember too the words of Jesus: 'You received without
charge, give without charge' (Mt 10:8). So we transmit by word
and example to others what has been given to us, while accepting that all authority in heaven and on earth has been given to
Jesus.

The gift of faith, according to Jesus, has been freely given to
us. Yet, in a sense, it comes with a price attached. Jesus' suffering and death was the price of our salvation and, consequently,
when we were baptised we assumed the duty of spreading the
faith. His last words on earth, immediately before his ascension
to heaven, were a missionary statement instructing his followers
to go into the whole world to lead converts to the Church.

For meditation
All authority in heaven and on earth has been given to me. (Mt
28:18)

Seventh Sunday of Easter
Gospel reading: John 17:1-11

Reflection

During his farewell speech to his disciples, when his earthly ministry was nearing completion, Jesus began to pray unashamedly in their presence. He prayed for himself as well as for them. There is a clear indication in the gospel text that he had begun praying: 'After saying this, Jesus raised his eyes to heaven and said' (Jn 17:1). This is the introductory phrase to what biblical scholars have described as the priestly prayer of Jesus.

This particular prayer of Jesus is one of the few instances in the gospels where the content of his prayer is revealed to us. During the prayer, he disclosed an intimate relationship with his Father, one that was based on familiarity and trust. Thus Jesus was able to say: 'Father, the hour has come: glorify your Son so that your Son may glorify you; and, through the power over all mankind that you have given him, let him give eternal life to all those you have entrusted to him' (Jn 17:1-2).

Significantly, the prayer did not focus only on himself and his relationship with his Father. Jesus also interceded powerfully for his disciples. For example, he said: 'Holy Father, keep those you have given me true to your name, so that they may be one like us' (Jn 17:11). Because prayer was central to the life of Jesus, and because he taught his disciples that it must be central in their lives, it is worth reflecting on the role of prayer in our lives.

Prayer is essentially time spent with God. It is a time when we can talk to him and bring our worries and needs into his presence. We can ask him questions and seek clarifications about all kinds of concerns. By spending time with him we learn more about him and we begin to know him personally.

As Christians, we are invited to spend regular time developing a personal relationship with God, especially his Son Jesus. This is prayer and, according to the *Catechism of the Catholic Church* (quoting Saint John Damascene), prayer is a 'raising of one's mind and heart to God'.

So prayer happens whenever we talk to God. It is fundamentally the expression of the relationship that exists between God and each one of us. It also expresses our communal relationship with God as members of the Church. When we pray properly, we listen attentively to what God is saying to us. In prayer we participate in God's life so that the remainder of our day is blessed with God's presence.

Prayer involves discernment, the discernment of God's will for our daily lives. Genuine prayer teaches us to listen in obedience to the promptings of the Holy Spirit and to be open to the change that is necessary in our lives, especially our turning away from sin, if we are to be authentic disciples. True prayer, therefore, empowers us to live virtuous lives. There are instances of convicted criminals who, for example, claim that God told them to commit murder. This cannot possibly be true. These people are deluded because genuine prayer makes us grow in holiness, not in hatred or in wrong-thinking morality.

Ultimately, prayer is about friendship with God. Through prayer, like the first disciples, we recognise Jesus as the Lamb of God, the Messiah, the risen Lord. But prayer, like any other relationship, does not just happen. We have to work at it, occasionally with trials and difficulties. However, our perseverance will be effective and we will discover meaning and the purpose in life.

In what ways do we pray each day? We cannot develop a mature relationship and friendship with God unless we explore and express that relationship regularly. When we truly pray, we communicate with God, thereby raising our minds and hearts in faith and hope. Prayer needs to be a priority in all our lives so that we can know God and so that our souls can seek sanctity.

For meditation
And eternal life is this: to know you, the only true God, and Jesus Christ whom you have sent. (Jn 17:3)

Pentecost Sunday
Gospel reading (Vigil): John 7:37-39
Gospel reading (Mass during the Day): John 20:19-23

Reflection

Jesus did not abandon his apostles, even when departing from this world to return to his Father in heaven. Ten days later, at Pentecost, one of his most significant promises – the promise to send the Holy Spirit in abundance on them – was extraordinarily realised.

After Pentecost the apostles were never again the same. The outpouring of the Holy Spirit impacted dramatically on their convictions and on their enthusiasm to carry out Jesus' wishes. The effects were immediately noticeable to the watching and listening crowds.

The apostles were filled with the Holy Spirit and given the gift of speech. As they spoke, their listeners – many of whom were foreigners – could hear and understand them in their own languages. The apostles now acted as members of a united and committed community. Although Christ had established the Church while still on earth, at Pentecost it became manifest in the world for the first time. It became obvious that God was working powerfully through the Church.

At Pentecost the Church earnestly began its mission to the whole world. This mission centres on preaching about the saving name of Jesus and about the wonders of God. God's greatest wonder is that, through the suffering and death of Jesus the Messiah, people are saved from the consequences of their sins: alienation from God.

Jesus' fundamental promise to his apostles was that they would never be without his presence and his help. He knew that they would be unable to contribute successfully to the universal mission that he had given them unless he sent the Holy Spirit. The Holy Spirit would bring courage to his disciples, and restore unity and harmony between people. There is evidence of this in John's Gospel when Jesus, after rising from the dead, said to his apostles: 'Receive the Holy Spirit. For those whose sins you forgive, they are forgiven; for those whose sins you retain, they are retained' (Jn 20:22-23).

Significantly, the outpouring of the Holy Spirit on the Church at its beginning corresponds to the earlier coming of the Holy Spirit on Jesus at the beginning of his public ministry when he was baptised in the River Jordan. In the same way that Jesus was always accompanied and guided by the Holy Spirit during his earthly life, so too is his Church as it brings repentant sinners to him. Repentance is necessary for salvation.

The feast of Pentecost celebrates a promise realised. It acknowledges that the Holy Spirit is at the heart of the Church's life. Because that is so, the Church cannot ultimately fail in its task of witnessing to Jesus' death and resurrection. It will eventually succeed in communicating the message of God's salvation to everyone in the world.

The sacrament of confirmation, which celebrates the outpouring of the Holy Spirit in our lives and is the sealing of the graces given in baptism, is our personal Pentecost experience when we are transformed into witnesses to the teaching and example of Jesus and his Church. We willingly take on the responsibility to share our Catholic faith with others.

The Feast of Pentecost is a wonderful celebration of the missionary Church. Let us reflect on our missionary efforts in our homes, schools and workplaces. How are we willing to demonstrate that we are serious about our confirmation (Pentecost) responsibilities? In what ways do we explain the authentic teaching of the Church? How do we experience Pentecost as a promise realised in our lives, leading us to make the urgency of the gospel message of salvation a reality for everyone we meet?

For meditation
As the Father sent me, so am I sending you. (Jn 20:21)

Some Feasts of the Lord in Ordinary Time

The Most Holy Trinity
Gospel reading: John 3:16-18

Reflection

Talking about God is invariably difficult because we need to use finite language and concepts to describe that which is infinite. When describing God, we are essentially describing the indescribable.

The most serious problem frustrating our reflection and discussion is the problem of religious language. Because human language is unable to express the totality of the mystery of God, we frequently resort to using images, metaphors and analogies when speaking about God. Human words are always necessarily limited.

Christian faith believes that there is one God, accepting that God is unique and indivisible. Accordingly, God is Supreme Being who is beyond description and on which all else depends. God is unchanging, all-powerful and all-knowing. God is often described rather impersonally as the Unmoved Mover and the Ground of Being. Saint Anselm (1033-1109AD) argued that God is 'that than which nothing greater can be conceived'. Thus God is beyond, separate and remote from nature, history and humanity. God transcends human and earthly reality.

Yet, God is also referred to in a very personal way as the God of Abraham, Isaac and Jacob (see Gen 32:9), who is unconditionally loving and merciful. God even reveals a personal name, *YHWH*, to Moses (see Exod 3) and has an affinity with his people. God is so close to creation and his people that his abiding presence is with them. The principal manifestation of God's intimacy is the partnership relationship that he has with his people, whereby he is their God and they are his people.

The simultaneous remoteness and familiarity of God provide Christians with a real dilemma because the terms are mutually exclusive in human reasoning. God's unity and uniqueness are stressed throughout the Old Testament. However, the fuller self-revelation of God's nature is not revealed until the New Testament account of the Incarnation.

Unlike Judaism and Islam, which also claim to believe in one God, revelation teaches Christians that, at the Incarnation, God became human, adopting our human nature, in the person of Jesus Christ. John's Gospel records that 'the Word was made flesh, he lived among us' (Jn 1:14) and that God established the closest possible relationship with humankind in Christ who is both divine and human. Consequently, Christians cannot speak about God without also referring to Christ. This is the uniqueness of the Christian perspective on revelation.

The Holy Spirit enables us to be in communion with Christ, yet the Holy Spirit has been active from the beginning of creation. The Holy Spirit mediates revelation, enkindles faith and nourishes the life of grace. Jesus revealed the Holy Spirit and promised to send it to his followers. This promise was fulfilled on Pentecost and the Holy Spirit still remains with the Church, keeping it holy and faithful to God's revelation.

For Christians, God is loving and merciful and has been revealed as Three-Persons-in-One: Father and Son and Holy Spirit. On Trinity Sunday, we recognise the most fundamental mystery of Christianity and we worship God who is Father and Son and Holy Spirit. Glory be to the Father and to the Son and to the Holy Spirit, as it was in the beginning, is now, and ever shall be.

For meditation
God sent his Son into the world not to condemn the world, but so that through him the world might be saved. (Jn 3:17)

The Body and Blood of Christ
Gospel reading: John 6:51-58

Reflection

On the Feast of the Body and Blood of Christ, it is appropriate to reflect on three essential Catholic teachings about the Eucharist: the link between the Eucharist and the Church, the Eucharist as sacrifice, and the Eucharist as Real Presence.

First, there is an intrinsic link between the Eucharist and the Church. Sharing the Eucharist requires belonging to the Church and *vice versa*. Understanding such a relationship between the Eucharist and the Church, which is central to Catholic teaching, has serious implications for people who receive Holy Communion.

There is a necessary connection between what Catholics do when they assemble for the celebration of Mass and what they do as members of the Church in other aspects of their daily lives. If they do not perceive such a connection, then it is probable that there will be many areas of inconsistency with gospel values and Catholic doctrine in their lifestyles.

The Church is most truly itself when it celebrates the Eucharist. But this truth presumes a unity between what Catholics say they believe and how they live. So faith and morality are inextricably bound up and we need to live in religious and moral harmony with the Church if we are to celebrate the Eucharist authentically.

The reception of Holy Communion implies that a person is in full communion with the Catholic Church and its beliefs. Receiving Communion is a sign of unity in faith and love with both the local church (and the local bishop) and the universal Church (and the Pope). While there are members of other ecclesial communities – various other Christian denominations seeking to follow Christ – who often wish to receive Holy Communion in Catholic churches and who argue that, because of our common belief in the divinity of Christ, we are, in a sense, in communion, the Catholic Church teaches that this communion is imperfect because it is incomplete. Hence there is genuine difficulty about Eucharistic sharing between Catholics and other Christians. But this does not deny that elements of holiness and truth are evident in other Christian communities.

Secondly, the Eucharist is a sacrifice. When the Eucharist is celebrated, the once-for-all sacrifice of Christ becomes effectively present for his people who are members of his Body, the Church. In describing the Eucharist as a sacrifice, the Catholic Church is not – as many other Christian traditions have often interpreted – denying the unique saving work of Jesus Christ when he died on Calvary.

There is a need for a renewed emphasis on the sacrificial understanding of the Eucharist among Catholics because such an understanding is at the very heart of the Eucharist. Traditionally, the Eucharist has never been understood merely as a service. No service can replace the sacrifice of the Mass. This is because the sacrifice of the Mass is the unbloody re-presentation of Christ's once-for-all sacrifice on Calvary.

Thirdly, Catholic faith accepts that the 'real' and 'substantial' presence of Christ is found in the Eucharist in the sense that the Eucharist is the supreme form of Christ's presence and his inner reality. This belief that Christ is truly present in the Eucharist, that there has been a change in the substances of bread and wine into the Body, Blood, Soul and Divinity of Christ, provides the basis and the imperative for adoration of and reverence for the reserved Blessed Sacrament. This is why Catholics are exhorted to spend time praying before the Blessed Sacrament.

Jesus Christ is the Bread of Life. He is the Living Bread that has come down from heaven to give life to the world (see Jn 6:51). Whoever eats the Bread of Life will have eternal life.

How do we deal with this basic Catholic teaching about the Eucharist? The teaching of the Church is the teaching of Christ. Can we, therefore, accept and believe the Church's teaching about the Eucharist? The Church teaches that the Eucharist is the summit of the Christian life. It is appropriate, then, when receiving Holy Communion, to repeat the prayer of one of the multitude following Jesus: 'I do have faith. Help the little faith I have' (Mk 9:23).

For meditation

I am the living bread which has come down from heaven. Anyone who ears this bread will live forever; and the bread that I shall give is my flesh for the life of the world. (Jn 6:51)

Sundays in Ordinary Time

Second Sunday in Ordinary Time
Gospel reading: John 1:29-34

Reflection

Two central characters, Jesus and John the Baptist, dominate the opening chapter of John's Gospel. (The gospel was written by John the Apostle and Evangelist, not to be confused with John the Baptist who features in the gospel.) The chapter reveals the essential aspects of Jesus' identity. He is the Word made flesh and the Lamb of God. Both are crucial for an understanding of who he is and what he does.

The first of the characters is Jesus. In the chapter, John the Baptist is quoted as having made one of the most remarkable professions of faith that is recorded in the New Testament. During his preaching, on seeing Jesus in the distance, he said to his listeners: 'Look, there is the lamb of God that takes away the sin of the world' (Jn 1:29). But John's profession of faith did not stop with that affirmation of Jesus. He elaborated further and then concluded: 'Yes, I have seen and I am the witness that he is the Chosen One of God' (Jn 1:24).

The Baptist's reference to Jesus as the Lamb of God brings to mind several images. Like other people of that time, the Baptist would have been familiar with the prophecies about the future Messiah, so he could have been referring to the servant of the Lord in chapter 53 of the Book of Isaiah, where the servant was presented as the one who would bring salvation to God's people by bearing their sufferings and sorrows.

In addition, there the servant was compared to a lamb being led to the slaughter house. So Jesus' identity could be understood in that context. The first chapter of John's Gospel focuses on the fulfilment of the Old Testament prophecies, all of which prepare for the Incarnation: the Word of God made flesh in Jesus.

The Baptist undoubtedly would also have been referring to the paschal lamb in chapter 12 of the Book of Exodus, who had effectively saved the Israelites from annihilation at the time of their escape from slavery in Egypt.

And the Baptist would have been referring too to the story of Abraham's binding of his son, Isaac, in chapter 22 of the Book of Genesis, where God provided the sacrificial lamb thereby saving Isaac from death. The Baptist, who had long been preparing to announce the Messiah's arrival, would have had all these scripture passages in mind when referring to Jesus as the Lamb of God.

It is clear that John the Baptist had a definite understanding of Jesus' identity by using the image of the lamb. Jesus would be the one to destroy sin and thus bring salvation to the world. The Baptist wanted to make clear the distinction between the Saviour and himself, whose task was to prepare the people for the great saving work of Jesus.

In that context, we are reminded of the words spoken by the priest before the distribution of Holy Communion at Mass: 'This is the Lamb of God who takes away the sins of the world. Happy are those who are called to his supper.' We remember the details of the apparition of Our Lady at Knock in Ireland, where the central figure in the apparition was the Lamb of God, the innocent victim suffering for our sins, at the altar surrounded by angels, with Mary, Saint Joseph and Saint John the Evangelist prayerfully looking on.

Thus the second character in chapter 1 of John's Gospel is John the Baptist. He described himself as a 'witness that he [Jesus] is the Chosen One of God' (Jn 1:34). The Baptist played a unique role in preparing the way for Jesus the Messiah to come into people's lives. He did this by his faithful witnessing and his penitential lifestyle.

We too are called to be witnesses to the Lamb of God and, by our convictions and lifestyle, to facilitate his arrival in the hearts and souls of those we meet and know. But to do that, we need to recognise Jesus as the Lamb of God. Let us pray that, like John the Baptist, we will always do so.

For meditation

A man is coming after me who ranks before me because he existed before me. I did not know him myself, and yet it was to reveal him to Israel that I came baptising with water. (Jn 1:30-31)

Third Sunday in Ordinary Time
Gospel reading: Matthew 4:12-23

Reflection

Jesus devoted his public ministry to preaching about the nearness of the kingdom of heaven and to inviting people to become his disciples. His lifestyle was guided completely by God's will and he challenged his listeners to accept God's will in their lives by rejecting sin and being faithful to his teaching.

As we reflect on Jesus' preaching, his most important message is repentance for our sins. In other words, Jesus challenges us to turn away from the darkness of sin so that we can live in the light of God's loving presence. Sin alienates us from the kingdom of heaven. Repentance demands humility and a fundamental change of heart. Otherwise we cannot truly be Jesus' disciples.

Central to repentance is genuine sorrow for our sins. Authentic sorrow is an outward manifestation of the inner journey of conversion. Unfortunately, however, we use the word 'sorry' so often and so carelessly that our sincerity is questionable. What, then, does it really mean to say 'I am sorry'?

To be sorry means to be sorrowful or saddened. Saying that we are sorry for having caused offence and hurt acknowledges that we are saddened because of the wrong that we have done and the hurt that we have caused. Significantly, we are saddened not only because we have offended God or hurt another person but also because we have diminished our own dignity as people made in the image and likeness of God.

If we have no sense of the harm that we have caused when we say that we are sorry, or if we have no intention of changing our behaviour in the future, then our sorrow is insincere because it is incomplete. We cannot claim to be motivated and guided by God's will if we are not repentant disciples.

When we celebrate the sacrament of reconciliation sincerely, by confessing our sins and being sorry for them, we demonstrate that we are humble and repentant. We express sorrow for our sins, knowing that God forgives us as we are absolved from our sins. God also gives us the grace and strength to resist temptation and avoid sin. Then our sorrow turns into joy.

Are there any occasions when we are saddened by what we have said or done to another person? Is it easy for us to say 'Sorry', or is it difficult for us to do? Valuing and appreciating forgiveness requires sorrow. We have the opportunity of celebrating God's forgiveness sacramentally by going to confession and acknowledging our sorrow.

Repentance is central to our lives as Jesus' disciples. Therefore, let our prayer be: Lord God, teach us to be repentant. Encourage us to change our minds and to soften our hardened hearts whenever we offend you and hurt other people. May we realise that, in doing so, we also diminish our own dignity. Help us always, through repentance, to return to your love by changing the direction of our lives and being faithful to your Son's teaching.

For meditation
Repent, for the kingdom of heaven is close at hand. (Mt 4:17)

Fourth Sunday in Ordinary Time
Gospel reading: Matthew 5:1-12

Reflection

The Sermon on the Mount in Matthew's Gospel is one of the most famous sermons in human history, although, interestingly, Matthew himself does not call it a sermon. For him, it is a more a presentation of Jesus' essential teachings about Christian discipleship and a development of what had already been revealed about human behaviour in the Hebrew scriptures.

Nonetheless, the sermon's significance is known to all Christians and its practical ideals for good living are well known outside Christianity. It begins with what have traditionally been called the Beatitudes, which offer a recipe for a proper and fulfilling life. The Beatitudes or Blessings (there are eight of them in Matthew's Gospel) provide an insightful introduction to the sermon and also summarise its contents.

The setting for the Beatitudes was important. According to the gospel text, Jesus 'went up the hill' where 'he sat down' and 'began to speak' (Mt 5:1-2). There was a formality to Jesus' actions. His going up the hill was reminiscent of Moses climbing Mount Sinai from where he delivered the Ten Commandments. Similarly, Jesus' sitting down and speaking were typical of the deliberate and authoritative way that a Jewish rabbi would act when teaching – somewhat like when the Pope speaks *ex cathedra.*

The qualities or traits listed in the Beatitudes are quite challenging. It is difficult to be poor in spirit, gentle, mournful, hungry and thirsty for what is right, merciful, pure in heart, peacemaking and persecuted in the cause of right. Most of us – unless we are saints – find it impossible to be virtuous in all these ways, at least while relying merely on our own efforts.

However, the promised rewards make the challenges worthwhile: the kingdom of heaven, the earth for our heritage, comfort, satisfaction, the reception of mercy, seeing God, being children of God and, again, the kingdom of heaven. All of the challenges and rewards are then summarised: 'Happy are you when people abuse you and persecute you and speak all kinds of calumny against you on my account. Rejoice and be glad, for your reward will be great in heaven' (Mt 5:11-12).

Relying on our own efforts, we will not be able to live up to this perfect model of behaviour but, with the help of God's grace, we will succeed in doing so. The basic Christian challenge is to respond to the graces given to us by God to reach the gospel perfection: 'You must therefore be perfect just as your heavenly Father is perfect' (Mt 5:48).

On reflection, the Beatitudes are a description of the character traits of Jesus himself. Thus they are an invitation to us to imitate his teaching and example in our daily lives so that, with his help and grace, we can become more like him – and perfect as our heavenly Father is perfect. If we could adopt such attitudes, we would have achieved what God has asked us to do in preparation for eternity.

For meditation
Happy are those who are persecuted in the cause of right: theirs is the kingdom of heaven. (Mt 5:10)

Fifth Sunday in Ordinary Time
Gospel reading: Matthew 5:13-16

Reflection

The gospel reading invites us to reflect on the significance of the light of Christ in our lives. The image of worldly light is used to communicate the deeper meaning of the light of Christ. Light dispels darkness. It gives us confidence because it points us in the right direction. It enables us to see things as they are.

We often take light for granted. Usually we do not notice it until, suddenly, we are without it. Whenever we experience power-failures we are reminded that we are particularly dependent on light for clear vision and we realise how necessary light is in our everyday lives. The real value of light, then, is to be found in its brightness, which provides us with direction.

Jesus used the image of light when speaking to his disciples. He told them that they were the light of the world, just as he was their light. By imitating his teaching and example in their own lives they could, like light, offer guidance and direction to other people. This was because they knew where they were going. The disciples were to share and reflect the light of Christ, which would give light to the world.

What is the light of Christ? The light of Christ is our guiding light. We feel secure in the light of Christ as it directs us through life. It is the teaching of Christ that motivates us to live in imitation of him. The light of Christ is God sharing his life and love with us. It is the life of Christ that is shared with us in the Eucharist: the living bread that has come down from heaven giving life to the world.

The light of Christ offers people meaning and hope. It highlights the love that can be found in the goodness of life. It challenges us to live God-like lives, lives without sin. It offers us consolation and reassurance because it assures us that Christ is near at all times.

We are as much disciples of Jesus as those to whom he spoke in the gospel. Each one of us is being challenged to be the light of the world. But we are also being commissioned collectively, as members of Christ's Church, to be the light of the world. We are the light of the world when we are decent and respectful towards other people and when we live according to the teaching of Christ and his Church. We are invited to see in a new light.

Seeing in a new light is about seeing in a new perspective, God's perspective. It is about behaving in a different way. Therefore, let us see in a different light and let our light shine in people's sight, so that, seeing our good works, they may give praise to our Father in heaven.

For meditation
You are the light of the world. (Mt 5:14)

Sixth Sunday in Ordinary Time

Gospel reading: Matthew 5:17-37

Reflection

People frequently refer to the Sermon on the Mount as being the New Law, replacing the Old Law, and the impression given is that, with Jesus, the rules have been somewhat loosened. Now it can be said that it is love that counts and that the rules take second place. But the error of this opinion is quickly evident when we check the eight Beatitudes at the beginning of the Sermon. Far from making life easier, the Sermon is even more demanding than the Old Law.

As God gradually revealed himself to the Chosen People, they began to understand that he loved them and wanted them to enjoy life in the land that he had given to them. In order for this to happen, they were to heed the warnings of the prophets and be faithful to God's commandments.

Therefore, they must not kill. They must not steal. They must be faithful to their spouses and they must not envy their neighbour. Contrary to what some people suggest nowadays, the Chosen People understood that God wanted them to keep his laws because he loved them, and not because he wanted to make them wretched and unhappy.

We know this from God's revelation of his loving nature in biblical texts such as the beautiful story of Hosea, whose love for his prostitute wife was analogous to the love that God had for his headstrong and sinful people. Through the prophets, God continually reminded them of his love, even as he pulled them back from the brink of destruction on many occasions. Indeed, in chapter 5 of the Book of Deuteronomy, we read that it was from God's love that the Ten Commandments sprang. Before listing the commands, God reminded them: 'I am *YHWH* your God who brought you out of the land of Egypt, out of the house of slavery' (Deut 5:6).

During the Sermon on the Mount itself, Jesus told his listeners that he had not come to destroy the Law or the Prophets: 'Do not imagine that I have come to abolish the Law or the Prophets. I have come not to abolish but to complete them. I tell you solemnly, till heaven and earth disappear, not one dot, not one little stroke, shall disappear from the Law until its purpose is achieved' (Mt 5:17-18).

To understand the implication of this key statement of Jesus, we might reflect that he sought not the end of the Law, not its destruction, but its perfection. Hence in the Sermon, Jesus taught that it is no longer sufficient not to kill one's neighbour. In future, his disciples would be required to control their anger so that their thoughts were purified and perfected. One by one, this extension of the Ten Commandments to thoughts and motives as well as actions, is found throughout this unique Sermon.

Jesus reinforced the idea of Christian perfection by linking it to the worship of God. If his followers desired to approach the altar and, while there, remembered friction with another person or people, they would be expected to leave their gifts at the altar and go to be reconciled first. The lesson for us is clear. This is how seriously God views our human relationships. We cannot hate our neighbour and purport to love God. That is not possible.

A much overlooked exhortation in the Sermon concerns prevarication in speech: 'All you need say is "Yes" if you mean yes, "No" if you mean no; anything more than this comes from the evil one' (Mt 5:37).

The Sermon on the Mount, then, especially each of the Beatitudes, provides us with a rich mine of spiritual treasures that give us much food for meditation.

For meditation
For I tell you, if your virtue goes no deeper than that of the scribes and Pharisees, you will never get into the kingdom of heaven. (Mt 5:20)

Seventh Sunday in Ordinary Time
Gospel reading: Matthew 5:38-48

Reflection

We all like our friends and we want to remember their birthdays and other special occasions. If they need our help, we are glad to be able to lend a hand, offer a listening ear, share our time or give some useful advice.

In contrast, we are not quite so kind to the people we dislike. If we really dislike them, to the point of hatred, then we may be tempted to treat them unjustly or, at least, damage their character by slandering them and gossiping about them. For Christians, this type of behaviour is unthinkable, precisely because Jesus explicitly forbade it.

During his Sermon on the Mount, Jesus reminded his audience about the Old Law before taking them forward to the perfection of the New Law: 'You have learnt how it was said: You must love your neighbour and hate your enemy. But I say this to you: love your enemies and pray for those who persecute you' (Mt 5:43-44).

This perfection was always to be found in the Law of God although, until the coming of Christ, it was not properly understood by the Chosen People. But Jesus made it explicit. There could no longer be any mistaking the law of charity. If people wanted to follow Christ, they were required to love their enemies.

Jesus gave some practical examples of the love of enemies in action: 'If anyone hits you on the right cheek, offer him the other as well' (Mt 5:39). Crucially, Jesus taught why he wanted his disciples to love their enemies: 'For if you love those who love you, what right have you to claim any credit? Even the tax collectors do as much, do they not?' (Mt 5:46).

According to Jesus, this is not sufficient. If we are kind to our friends and hate our enemies, or even if, not hating them, we refuse to be charitable towards them, we are doing no more than the pagans do. There is no merit in that. If we want to please God, then we are obliged to do more. We are challenged by the gospel to behave decently towards those to whom we are not naturally attracted. In short, we must love our enemies.

This teaching, which is unique to Christianity, is a reflection of God's perfection. We know this because Jesus concluded this part of his sermon by exhorting his listeners to 'be perfect just as your heavenly Father is perfect' (Mt 5:48).

When we next receive a request for help, or when our opinion is sought from a neighbour or work colleague to whom we are not naturally drawn, let us remember Jesus' exhortation and respond with kindness and generosity. There is always someone, in every social context, who is not popular, or who is difficult and unattractive. It is to these people that we are asked to respond in true charity with a kind word, a small gift, perhaps, or an offer of friendship. That will reflect, somewhat, the perfection of God in a world full of selfishness and conflict.

For Meditation
Love your enemies and pray for those who persecute you. (Mt 5:44)

Eighth Sunday in Ordinary Time
Gospel reading: Matthew 6:24-34

Reflection

It is common today to meet people who are anxious about the future. They talk about planning their lives, their career plans and their holiday plans – often stretching forward for years to cover every possible situation. Usually, they are also quite worried about financial and other material considerations.

Yet Jesus taught his disciples not to worry about such matters. He went as far as saying that nobody can serve both God and wealth: 'No one can be the slave of two masters: he will either hate the first and love the second, or treat the first with respect and the second with scorn' (Mt 6:24). The question for us, then, is: Which of the two do we love – God or wealth?

Wealth comprises money, property and all material things. If our lives and plans are centred around how much money we have, or our position on the property ladder, then we are not living in accordance with Jesus' teaching.

He taught clearly and with great beauty that we are not to worry about material things: 'That is why I am telling you not to worry about your life and what you are to eat, nor about your body and how you are to clothe it. Surely life means more than food, and the body more than clothing! Look at the birds in the sky. They do not sow or reap or gather into barns; yet your heavenly Father feeds them. Are you not worth much more than they are?' (Mt 6:25-26).

That is one reason why we trust in God's providence. He will provide for all our needs. But there is another important reason, according to Jesus, why it is futile – and unchristian – to worry about material things: 'Can any of you, for all his worrying, add one single cubit to his span of life?' (Mt 6:27). Then again, in one of the most moving passages of scripture, Jesus taught: 'Think of the flowers growing in the fields; they never have to work or spin; yet I assure you that not even Solomon in all his regalia was robed like one of these' (Mt 6:28-29).

These words of Jesus about the providence of God are very powerful. They help us to recognise how far many of us have moved from placing the realm of the spiritual at the centre of our lives. Increasing numbers of people go along with the modern mindset where money, property and careers – wealth – have become more important than God. Jesus described this materialism as lack of faith: 'Now if that is how God clothes the grass in the field which is there today and thrown into the furnace tomorrow, will he not much more look after you, you people of little faith?' (Mt 6:30).

The essence of genuine Christian living is to place our lives in the hands of God. We are continually invited to listen to Jesus' exhortation not to worry about material things, which rot, die and can be replaced. We certainly cannot take them with us when we leave this world, and so it is foolish to worry about them.

God our Father knows our every need. This is what Jesus said: 'Set your hearts on [the Father's] kingdom first, and on his righteousness, and all these other things will be given you as well' (Mt 6:33). It is pointless to waste time worrying about tomorrow when we know that 'tomorrow will take care of itself. Each day has enough trouble of its own' (Mt 6:34).

For meditation
You cannot be the slave of both God and money. (Mt 6:24)

Ninth Sunday in Ordinary Time
Gospel reading: Matthew 7:21-27

Reflection

A well-known and often used cliché is: Even ears have walls. This means that we can obstruct our ears to avoid engaging with what may upset us or challenge us. Sometimes, while we hear what other people say, we may not let them communicate with us. We may refuse to allow their message to register. Metaphorically speaking, we close our ears to the message being conveyed by 'letting it in one ear and out the other'. In doing so, we choose to remain unmoved and indifferent to what is being said.

There is a real and significant difference between listening and hearing. Hearing is the physiological response to external noise or sound. We do not engage with the sound. We do not dialogue with the message that is being communicated. Consequently, we are not open to the possibility of change in our lives. We merely register the sound as we hear it and do nothing further. For instance, how often have we heard the news headlines on radio and, five minutes later, not been able to recall them? Hearing does not demand attention.

In contrast, listening requires engagement with sound. It demands action in response to the message. When we listen, we remember. We are open to the possibility of changing our lives because of the message being communicated. Our attitudes and actions may become different. Basically, we allow the sound and, more importantly the message it communicates, to challenge us. An example is when we vary our diet because our medical doctor warns us that failing to do so would seriously jeopardise our health. Listening involves attentiveness and sensitivity.

Recently, a woman said to me: 'My husband hasn't listened to me for thirty years.' Obviously, he had heard her speaking every day. But he had rarely devoted serious consideration to what she said. He had never engaged with her attempts at communication because he had not been listening. Whenever they argued, he would say: 'I'm not listening.' Therefore, their relationship had never developed to its full potential.

The same may happen in our relationships with God. Many of us hear God's word regularly, but may rarely listen to it because we do not want to be disturbed and inconvenienced by its challenging message. To do so would unsettle our attitudes and lifestyle. One proof is that, if we were to ask Mass-goers what the gospel reading was about ten minutes after Mass, few would remember. If we do not listen attentively to the word of God we cannot know how God is asking us to change our lives. Then we may not allow the teaching and example of Christ to influence our decisions.

There is a difference between hearing and listening. Jesus assures us that, if we listen to his word, our faith will be founded on rock. Our relationship with God will mature. In what ways do we listen to the word of God? Let us remember that even ears have walls!

For meditation
Everyone who listens to these words of mine and acts on them will be like a sensible man who built his house on rock. (Mt 7:24)

Tenth Sunday in Ordinary Time
Gospel reading: Matthew 9:9-13

Reflection

Jesus had a strange effect on some people. When he said to them 'Follow me', they simply followed him. Surprisingly, they did not hesitate. Following him seemed perfectly natural and there was no delay in their response to his invitation. It marked the beginning of a relationship with him.

However, Jesus' invitation was not just an invitation to walk beside him. It was an invitation to a new way of life. His invitation was a call to radical transformation. Jesus called people, they often followed him immediately and, usually, their lives were changed forever. They became his disciples. According to Jesus' teaching, discipleship involved striving for wholeness through commitment to God's word and commandments.

If a stranger walking past us on the street asked us to follow him, we would probably assume that he was daft. We certainly would not follow the stranger. Yet, as baptised Christians, everyday Jesus asks us to follow him. He may not physically pass us on the street, but we meet him in our hearts when we pray, in other people, and in the Church's teaching and sacraments.

Like those in the gospel who responded to his invitation, we are Jesus' disciples. Similarly, discipleship for us is about striving for wholeness through our commitment to God's commandments. It is about entering a relationship of trust and obedience with Jesus that truly distinguishes us as his brothers and sisters. Discipleship involves total commitment to the gospel. Half-hearted commitment – which, admittedly, is tempting – is never sufficient.

Christian discipleship is costly. It demands that we put the needs of other people before our own. This often involves 'going against the grain'. Everyday we are challenged to undergo radical conversion from being selfish to being selfless. Our commitment to the Good News needs to be resolute. In this way we achieve perfection and become perfect as our heavenly Father is perfect. This is what Jesus instructed his disciples to do. Such perfection can only be achieved through total commitment.

Jesus' call to discipleship is not selective. It is for everyone, especially those who feel unworthy for whatever reasons. He came to save sinners. All of us are sinners and, in saving us from the consequences of our sins, he invites us to join his new way of life.

The basic Christian call is the call to discipleship. Jesus' invitation 'Follow me' sounds simple. In practice, however, it is demanding because it challenges us to abandon our sinful past. Our response is not invited just at baptism but we are asked to renew that response every day. The gospel invites us to re-order our priorities so that they imitate the priorities of Christ. Only then will we truly be his disciples. Let us listen for Jesus' invitation to follow him and renew our commitment everyday.

For meditation
I did not come to call the virtuous, but sinners. (Mt 9:13)

Eleventh Sunday in Ordinary Time
Gospel reading: Matthew 9:36 – 10:8

Reflection

Jesus' summoning of the Twelve occurred in the context of his pity for the crowds of people who were 'harassed and dejected, like sheep without a shepherd' (Mt 9:36). The people were leaderless. They needed guidance and Jesus taught them.

Jesus always practised what he preached. Thus he responded compassionately to their various needs, bringing them healing and reconciliation. While his response usually included attention to their physical and emotional needs, it was also spiritual and concerned with eternal life.

The task given to the Twelve by Jesus provided the basis for the Church's missionary character. Matthew's Gospel records that, as they were commissioned by Jesus, they were given 'authority over unclean spirits with power to cast them out and cure all kinds of diseases and sickness' (Mt 10:1). (Perhaps this was a prefiguring of what the apostles and their successors would subsequently do when celebrating the sacraments.) They were specifically sent to 'the lost sheep of the House of Israel' to 'proclaim that the kingdom of heaven is close at hand' (Mt10:6-7).

Initially, the Twelve were sent only to the Jewish communities. It was as if they were undergoing training and reporting back to Jesus before being entrusted with the even greater task of bringing the Good News about him and salvation to the ends of the earth, as we read in chapter 28 of Matthew's Gospel and chapter 1 of the Acts of the Apostles.

The Twelve symbolise the Church, which was founded on the apostles and which is the people of the New Covenant just as the old People of God, the nation of Israel, was descended from the twelve patriarchs. The Church was established to continue the work of Jesus after he had ascended to the Father, having redeemed us from the consequences of sin by his suffering and death.

The Church's task was essentially to be missionary. It was to spread the name of Jesus Christ throughout the entire world and bring his mercy and forgiveness into the hearts and souls of all peoples. Its message was to be same as Jesus' message: the kingdom of God is close at hand.

Today the Church continues the mission of the Twelve. At baptism, all of us are given the task of being involved in its missionary activity by using every opportunity to share the name and message of Jesus with other people. Sometimes we mistakenly assume that involvement in the Church's mission is not for us because we are unable to travel to faraway countries. However, the Church's mission is wherever we are, whether in our homes or schools or workplaces, where we can be a positive influence. We do not have to go abroad to be missionaries.

The best way that we can be part of the Church's mission is by repenting for our sins and being faithful to the teaching of Christ and his Church. In this way we proclaim unequivocally that the kingdom of heaven in close at hand. There are many people around us who feel dejected and confused. They desperately need guidance, which we can offer by our encouraging and truthful words and by our good example that is firmly rooted in Christ. Then, like the Twelve, we will be unquestionably involved in the Church's mission.

For meditation
You received without charge, give without charge. (Mt 10:8)

Twelfth Sunday in Ordinary Time
Gospel reading: Matthew 10:26-33

Reflection

'Do not be afraid' (Mt 10:26). Where have we heard these words before? They are quite familiar to most of us because they have been quoted often by preachers and commentators since the death of Pope John Paul II in 2005. A recurrent theme from the beginning of his pontificate in 1978 was: Do not be afraid.

This was also John Paul's message to Catholics and to the entire world as he passed from this life to eternal life. His entire life, and especially his final illness, demonstrated that he himself was fearless because of his absolute faith and trust in the person and saving message of Jesus Christ. And he urged everyone else to have the same conviction.

John Paul was not the first person to say 'Do not be afraid'. In the Old Testament, God said it to the prophets. The angel Gabriel also spoke these words to Mary before telling her that she would become the Mother of the Saviour of the world. Years later, Jesus instructed the Twelve not to be afraid when he commissioned them to continue his work of proclaiming the Good News. The Good News was essentially that the kingdom of heaven was close and that people must undergo conversion from their sinful lives.

Jesus knew that this message, when preached and lived by his disciples, would not always be welcomed. The disciples would frequently be ridiculed and rejected, as he had been. Discipleship would indeed be costly because it would require humility and sacrifice. Therefore, Jesus warned them to be convinced about their message and to be confident that God was with them in every situation. He assured them: 'If anyone declares himself for me in the presence of men, I will declare myself for him in the presence of my Father in heaven' (Mt 10:32).

Jesus says the same to us. The apostles were not living in easier times than ours. Yet they willingly suffered for the faith, never making excuses to dilute it or compromise its principles. Neither should we, believing that God loves and supports us in every crisis. Faith dispels fear.

As committed disciples, we are duty bound to proclaim the gospel fearlessly and confidently. This is our baptismal obligation. We are required to be prophetic people by speaking the truth at all times. We will frequently experience opposition and alienation because of our Christian beliefs and we will be tempted to abandon our commitment in order to remain popular. However, popularity in this life does not equate with good standing in the next life.

We can learn from the great heritage of our saints who, even in the face of persecution and martyrdom, did not hesitate to remain faithful to Christ and his teaching. They refused to deny him. Fortunately, most of us do not suffer the threat of martyrdom. Instead, we are asked to become fearless witnesses to Christ in all circumstances and to cope in a dignified manner with ridicule in our workplaces or disagreement among friends and colleagues, perhaps even our families. Let us pray that we will have the courage of our convictions and not be afraid.

For meditation
Do not be afraid of those who kill the body but cannot kill the soul; fear him rather who can destroy both body and soul in hell. (Mt 10:28)

Thirteenth Sunday in Ordinary Time
Gospel reading: Matthew 10:37-42

Reflection

Rocketing divorce rates and the now widespread practice of co-habitation in preference to marriage are two examples among numerous of the difficulty, especially in western societies, of people making lasting commitments to one another. Even many couples who claim to love each other are reluctant to make vows that bind them for life.

This apparent inability to make definitive commitments has also affected the priesthood and religious life. After the Second Vatican Council (1962-1965), many priests and religious abandoned their commitment in their droves. Nowadays it is not uncommon to hear the suggestion that priesthood and religious life should only be a temporary arrangement, that young people might commit to these lifestyles for a specified period of time and then be free to do other things.

Jesus was very clear about the commitment that he expects from his disciples: 'Anyone who prefers father or mother to me is not worthy of me. Anyone who prefers son or daughter to me is not worthy of me. Anyone who does not take his cross and follow in my footsteps is not worthy of me' (Mt 10:37-38). Christians are called to put Christ first. Total commitment, nothing less, is required.

In the scale of relationships, then, Christ is unquestionably first. Not even the closest of family relationships is more important than our relationship with Christ. Nothing less than total commitment is acceptable. The same applies in the case of suffering. Whatever sufferings come our way, whether physical illness or mental anguish or spiritual distress, we accept them for the love of Christ.

To underline the importance of nourishing this total commitment of his followers, Jesus promised rewards to those who give even a drink of water to those in need. It is incumbent on us, then, to re-examine our Christian commitment.

For example, how do we understand the obligation to attend Sunday Mass? For some of us, it may be based on a sort of turgid duty that arises from fear or guilt. For others, it may be due to an unreflected lifelong habit. Or it may be a result of our love of God and the desire to offer praise and worship in the context of a believing community.

If our religious observance is to be transformed into a duty of love, then we need to reflect carefully on the words of Jesus that no human being, nothing on the face of the earth, should be more important to us than him. Only when we appreciate the pre-eminence of Jesus in our lives, will everything else fall into its correct perspective.

For meditation
Anyone who welcomes you welcomes me; and those who welcome me welcome the one who sent me. (Mt 10:40)

Fourteenth Sunday in Ordinary Time
Gospel reading: Matthew 11:25-30

Reflection
God's self-revelation (self-disclosure) is truly a gift because without it we would know nothing about God's nature and interaction with us and the universe. We could not even begin to imagine the joy and the privilege of being in God's presence.

The fullness of God's self-revelation is found in the Incarnate Son of God. Jesus, through his life and ministry, teaches us that his Father is loving and redeeming. We learn that the Father never abandons us. He constantly calls us to return after we have turned away because of our sins. This is the essence of God's revelation.

Yet all people are not equally appreciative of God's revelation. Jesus thanked his Father for 'hiding these things from the learned and the clever and revealing them to mere children' (Mt 11:25). Ironically, it is lowly and humble people who best understand God's secrets.

Significantly, the wisdom that really matters is to be found among those whom the world judges to be unwise. Those who are considered 'learned' and 'clever' in worldly terms are often unwilling to accept God's providential care and his commandments. Instead, it is 'mere children', or rather those who have a childlike attitude towards God, who respond wholeheartedly to God's communication.

There is a significant difference between being childlike and being childish. To be childlike means to be trusting. It involves having a sense of wonder and awe. Those who have a childlike attitude appreciate simplicity and the blessedness of life's ordinary situations. When we are childlike we accept our dependence on God, knowing that we cannot be in complete control.

In contrast, to be childish means to be manipulative, demanding and immature. Childishness results from selfishness and an arrogant attitude of self-importance. It is not confined to children. In fact it is found much more often in adults. Childish people mistakenly presume that they are autonomous and that they can be in control of their lives without reference to other people and God.

For Christians, conversion involves changing from childish attitudes and behaviour to childlike trust and selflessness. Basically, conversion is about travelling the journey from sinfulness to saintliness. We need to change from being 'learned' and 'clever', always trying to be in control of life, to being 'mere children', graciously accepting our total dependence on God for everything. Only then can God teach us what he wants us to learn.

Infants instinctively trust their parents. It is perfectly natural. But as we grow older, we become quite independent of our parents and we often reject their values and good example. We may do the same with God. Perhaps we can learn to trust God again. We need to discard our childish ways and become more childlike so that we can experience the joy of being God's children again.

For meditation
Come to me, all you who labour and are overburdened, and I will give you rest. (Mt 11:28)

Fifteenth Sunday in Ordinary Time
Gospel reading: Matthew 13:1-23

Reflection

The setting for the parable of the sower is informative. Matthew tells us that Jesus was sitting by the lakeside when 'such crowds gathered round him' (Mt 13:2) that he went to a boat and sat in it while the multitudes stood on the shore. We can readily imagine this scene, with great crowds of people hurrying to where Jesus was, anxious to listen to him teaching about God.

Not many of us enjoy being pushed and crushed as tends to happen when there are crowds of people around us. So it tells us much about Jesus' popularity – and the attractiveness of his teaching – that the people were willing to suffer the discomfort of being part of a large crowd simply to hear him speak. Many of them would feel another kind of discomfort, though, as Jesus' parable unfolded.

Familiar with the agricultural theme, they would have listened attentively to Jesus and at least some of them would have understood. Just as a farmer sows seed, some of which comes to fruition but much of which does not for various reasons, so the word of God goes unheeded by people who are negligent or wilful in their selfish refusal to nurture the seed of faith that is given to them by God.

Jesus concluded the parable: 'Listen, anyone who has ears!' (Mt 13:9). In other words, those who truly seek God, those who want to understand, will hear God speaking to them through the parable.

We tend to think of the parabolic method as being aimed at making it easier for the listeners to understand the things of God, without having to think too much about the story. But these words of Jesus require serious reflection, as does the disciples' question to Jesus asking why he spoke to the crowd in parables.

Jesus responded: 'Because the mysteries of the kingdom of heaven are revealed to us, but they are not revealed to them' (Mt 13:11). Thus we come full circle, back to the purpose of the parables, which is to teach – in a hidden way – the truths of the faith.

In explaining the meaning of the parable of the sower, Jesus highlighted some important truths for us. For instance, he said:

'When anyone hears the word of God without understanding it, the evil one comes and carries off what was sown in his heart: this is the man who received the seed on the edge of the path' (Mt 13:19).

There is a clear message here for parents, priests, teachers and anyone who is involved in passing on the faith. Neglecting to educate those in our care, or neglecting to nurture the seed of faith planted in their souls at baptism so that they cannot understand it to the best of their ability, is a grave failing and a serious sin.

Similarly, the seed that fell on stony ground represents those who receive the faith with joy but buckle and fall away when trials come. Perhaps most of us fall into this category, by not living up to the demands of the Christian life because we are unwilling to suffer for Christ. Or perhaps we are like those who received the seed among thorns, that is, we allowed our faith to be choked because we preferred riches and the things of this world to following Christ.

The gospel message is always the same and the parable of the sower embodies the entire message: we need to put God first in our lives. Nothing can be allowed to prevent us from doing God's will. We strive to bring forth only good fruit in everything that we do and we do everything for the greater glory of God.

For meditation
But happy are your eyes because they see, your ears because they hear! (Mt 13:16)

Sixteenth Sunday in Ordinary Time
Gospel reading: Matthew 13:24-43

Reflection

During his ministry, Jesus preached that the kingdom of heaven was near. The kingdom of heaven is the reign of God. Jesus used several images when speaking about the kingdom since it is beyond complete description and explanation in human words.

Jesus inaugurated God's kingdom on this earth. We are already living in the kingdom because the Church is the seed and the beginning of the kingdom. But the Church is not itself the kingdom in all its fullness. The kingdom is a more inclusive reality than the Church of Christ and, similarly, the Church of Christ is a more inclusive reality than the Catholic Church. Many characteristics of the Church of Christ are also to be found outside the Catholic Church and various aspects of the kingdom occur outside the Church of Christ in other religions.

This is because the Catholic Church is not identical with either the Church of Christ or the kingdom. The Second Vatican Council (1962-1965) taught that the Church of Christ 'subsists' in the Catholic Church. This means that, although elements of sanctification and truth also occur outside the visible structures of the Catholic Church and beyond the wider boundaries of the Church of Christ, the fullness of grace and truth are entrusted by Christ to the Catholic Church. Thus there is an inextricable relationship between the Catholic Church, the Church of Christ and the kingdom of God.

The fullness of the kingdom is expected at the end of time. Meanwhile, the Church on earth is on a pilgrimage towards that end. The Church, the People of God, always has members who are sinners. Therefore, while unfailingly holy because Christ is its Head, the Church is constantly in need of purification and renewal. Only at the end of time will the Church on earth achieve fully the perfection to which it is called when the kingdom of God is fulfilled in heaven. Then the Church will be free from all sin.

In that respect, the Church is similar to a field of wheat. The field of wheat ripens slowly, requiring much care and patience from the farmer. Growth may seem undetectable but it occurs as the wheat matures and becomes ready for the harvest. Using the parable of the wheat and the darnel, Jesus teaches two important lessons. First, the Church includes both the good and the bad. Both co-exist. Awareness of God's reign emerges slowly but surely. Secondly, the good and the bad will be separated at harvest time. Judgement comes at the end.

The Church and the kingdom of God are absolutely linked. Active participation in the Church's life and mission prepares us well for judgement at the end of time. The parables about the kingdom challenge us to remain faithful to the Church's teaching and guidance, reminding us that the Church is the seed and the beginning of the kingdom here on earth. The Church, when it is faithful to its vocation, is the primary means whereby the kingdom is brought about.

For meditation
The sower of the good seed is the Son of Man. The field is the world; the good seed is the subjects of the kingdom; the darnel, the subjects of the evil one; the enemy who sowed them, the devil; the harvest is the end of the world; the reapers are the angels. (Mt 13:37-39)

Seventeenth Sunday in Ordinary Time
Gospel reading: Matthew 13:44-52

Reflection

It is not fashionable to talk about hell nowadays. Many people no longer believe in the reality of hell. Some people also deny the reality of heaven, arguing that there is nothing after life on this earth. Yet, according to the scriptures, the ultimate destiny of each human being will be either heaven or hell.

This is a fundamental teaching of Christianity. It is erroneous to presume, as many people do, that God will bring all people to heaven anyway, regardless of how they have lived, because the Creator's love and mercy have no limits – although, according to Saint Paul, God wants everyone to be saved (see 1 Tim 2:4).

God's love is indeed unconditional and his mercy is endless. But God gives each person the gift of free will and always respects that freedom. It is naïve to assume that our conscious decisions and freely-chosen actions do not have consequences.

In his preaching, Jesus was definite about the consequences of how we live on this earth. He taught that at the end of time there will be judgement when the angels will separate the wicked from the just. The wicked will then be thrown 'into the blazing furnace where there will be weeping and grinding of teeth' (Mt 13:50). They will be alienated from God forever, not because of God's harsh judgement but rather because of the self-imposed judgement of their sinful attitudes and lifestyles.

There is a connection between how we live in this world and our ultimate destiny in the next life. The two are undeniably linked. During our earthly lives we have many opportunities to learn how to know and love God. God is the Just Judge and Merciful Father who desires that we journey towards our true home in heaven by freely choosing to avoid sin and being faithful to the gospel.

If we knowingly and freely choose sinfulness and evil throughout our lives, without ever repenting, our eternal destiny will be alienation from God. We sin when we refuse to respond to God's loving presence in our lives and in our world. We also sin when we choose estrangement from God. While

God always invites us to return to his loving presence, he will not force us to do so.

How we choose to live in this world has a bearing on the next life. We cannot be with God for ever in heaven unless we are with him during this earthly life. We prepare for the next life – a life enjoying the eternal happiness of heaven – by living this life as fully as possible in the presence of God. We are challenged to be faithful to Christ's teaching and example, keeping his commandments.

The Church teaches us that hell exists. But it has never declared that there is anyone in there. Instead, it offers us access to God's life through its preaching of the word of God and the sacraments. So will it be heaven or will it be hell for eternity? We must choose.

For meditation

This is how it will be at the end of time: the angels will appear and separate the wicked from the just to throw them into the blazing furnace where there will be weeping and grinding of teeth. (Mt 13:49-50)

Eighteenth Sunday in Ordinary Time
Gospel reading: Matthew 14:13-21

Reflection

In the story of the loaves and fish, we learn about Jesus feeding the hungry crowd by multiplying five loaves and two fish. He did this because he was concerned for the people who had stayed with him and listened to him. In a sense, he was grateful to them for listening to him talking about the kingdom of heaven.

Initially, when his disciples advised him to send the people away, he challenged them to feed the crowd themselves. However, when they admitted that they were powerless, he taught and empowered them by example.

This is significant because Jesus always practised what he preached and he never asked others to do what he was unwilling to do himself. He satisfied the crowd's physical hunger and, in doing so, he enhanced the authority of what he had already said to them. Jesus had enough for everybody and still some remaining.

Interestingly, the multiplication of the loaves and fish is Jesus' only public miracle that is recorded in each of the four gospels, thus stressing its importance for the Christian community. The love and generosity of Jesus in tending to the needs of the hungry crowd offer us an insight into his own total self-giving for others at the Last Supper and in his suffering and death.

Jesus' miracle of the loaves and fish, which responded to the physical hunger of the crowd, foreshadowed his miracle at the Last Supper when he shared himself in the Eucharist – the Bread of Life – with his disciples, thereby satisfying their spiritual hunger.

The lesson of the miracle of the loaves and fish is obvious: by portraying Jesus as doing what God did for the Israelites in the desert, by giving them manna, the evangelist is forging an identity between Jesus and God. Jesus, who responded to and reached out to people in their need, wants his followers to do the same. The question for all of us is: In what ways do we share ourselves, our gifts and our time with other people when they are needy? In other words, what are we prepared to do to help people avoid sin and facilitate the salvation of their souls? We are challenged to appreciate one another just as Jesus appreciated the crowd that had gathered to listen to him.

It can be extremely difficult to put other people's needs before our own. However, that is what we are called to do as Christian disciples. In the miracle of the loaves and fish, Jesus relied on his Father's help as he responded to a crisis. Likewise, we, Jesus' disciples, need to rely on his help as we respond to crises and needs.

Can we, by our convictions and lifestyles, satisfy the hunger in other people's lives? In the same spirit, can we desist from asking other people to do what we are unwilling to do ourselves? Let us, therefore, give generously and receive graciously, always imitating the generosity of our Lord and Saviour Jesus Christ.

For meditation
They all ate as much as they wanted, and they collected the scraps remaining, twelve baskets full. (Mt 14:20)

Nineteenth Sunday in Ordinary Time
Gospel reading: Matthew 14:22-33

Reflection

Fear is very basic to our human condition. We are often full of fears, some of them irrational. So it might seem that, having just witnessed Jesus miraculously feed more than five thousand people (see Mt 14:15-21), Peter and the others were being irrational by expressing fear and anxiety when, in the midst of a storm at sea, Jesus walked towards their boat that was being tossed about by the wind.

But Peter was learning. His fear at finding himself in such a precarious position in the boat, while Jesus had gone up into the hills alone to pray, was somewhat abated when the apparition approaching them and, filling them with fear, offered this reassurance: 'Courage! It is I! Do not be afraid' (Mt 14:27). Peter was able to muster sufficient faith to respond: 'Lord, if it is you, tell me to come to you across the water' (Mt 14:28).

This was indeed a leap of faith. Already filled with fear at finding himself in the middle of a stormy sea in a small boat, with only other terrified followers of Jesus for company, Peter asked for no proof that Jesus was who he said he was. Peter sought a command that would permit him to exercise his faith.

Nonetheless, having bravely made this initial act of faith, Peter then began to doubt. The wind was raging around him and the waters were turbulent. He began to sink, and suddenly cried: 'Lord! Save me!' (Mt 14:30). The lesson for us here is that there is an ideal to follow when our own faith begins to crumble.

It is better, of course, not to doubt. Indulging in doubt has always been considered to be sinful by the Church. But if we fall, if we allow ourselves, like Peter, to doubt the power of Jesus momentarily – even to calm stormy seas – then let us immediately acknowledge that same power by asking for salvation, as Peter did.

Jesus responded to Peter's cry for help by stretching out a saving hand, while at the same time rebuking him for doubting: 'Man of little faith, why did you doubt?' (Mt 14:31).

This miracle teaches us about the supernatural character of the Church. If we think that the Church is a purely human institution, then we will be full of fear when it is tossed about on the winds of fashion and controversy. We will begin to doubt as Peter doubted. In that case, we must be prepared for the same rebuke given to Peter.

The truth is that Christ is in charge of his Church. Because of that, there is no reason for us to doubt. All that God asks of us is that we are faithful to him and to the teachings of his Church. Matthew's account of this miracle concludes with the news that when they were all gathered together in the boat, with Jesus, the storm ceased. When they recognised his power, calm was restored.

The lesson for us is simple. The Church, notwithstanding its sinful members and their weaknesses, is a divine-human institution. It relies on supernatural help to achieve its mission which is the salvation of the whole world. There is no need for us to be fearful.

For meditation
The men in the boat bowed down before him and said, 'Truly, you are the Son of God.' (Mt 14:33)

Twentieth Sunday in Ordinary Time
Gospel reading: Matthew 15:21-28

Reflection

There was a long history of conflict between the Israelites and the Canaanites. Over the years, the Canaanites were defeated and most of them fled the land. Some of them settled in Tyre and Sidon (Lebanon and Syria). It was here that Jesus met the woman in today's gospel reading.

Why, we may ask, did Jesus travel to this Gentile region, especially given the turbulent historical background? The most likely reason is that he had been in conflict with the Pharisees and other religious leaders, and he wanted to go away for a while, not least because he did not want the trouble with his enemies to escalate. That is one of the practical reasons for his venturing into Gentile territory at this time.

Jesus' spiritual and religious reasons seem clear. The Jewish leaders were battling with him, were jealous of him and were, in essence, rejecting him. So he turned his attention to the Gentiles – those who were not Jews. He entered Gentile territory at the very time the Jewish leaders rejected him, and a Gentile woman publicly recognised his power and authority. The contrast must have been clear to his followers.

The woman cried out to Jesus: 'Sir, Son of David, take pity on me. My daughter is tormented by a devil' (Mt 15:22). Her words are significant. She was aware of the historical animosity between the Jews and the Canaanites. Nevertheless, she expressed her belief in Jesus as the promised Messiah. It was astonishing that she should make that kind of acknowledgement, notwithstanding her anxiety to have her daughter healed.

At first Jesus was silent, perhaps testing her perseverance. She was not found wanting, following him and pleading with him. Jesus' silence was educational. He wanted his disciples and the woman to understand fully that he was the Son of David, the Messiah. The kingdom had to be offered to the Jews first, in fulfilment of the Old Testament prophecies.

However, the woman humbly knelt before Jesus and begged: 'Lord, help me' (Mt 15:25). Jesus continued to test her by reminding her about the historic enmity between her people, the

Canaanites, and the Chosen People, the Israelites. He told her that she was asking him to give privileges intended for the children (the Jews) to the house-dogs (the Gentiles).

The woman was not offended. She knew that the long awaited Messiah was a Jewish Messiah and that the Jews were the Chosen People. But she quipped that even the dogs ate the crumbs that fell from their master's table. In other words, although God's mercy is first for the Jews, surely some of it can be spared for the Gentiles. The Canaanite woman's words were a manifestation of real faith in Jesus, and were in stark contrast to the lack of faith of the Jewish leaders who rejected him. Jesus rewarded her faith by healing her daughter.

The account of Jesus' encounter with the Canaanite woman teaches us about the grace of God and about the trusting faith that is appropriate when we experience suffering. But there is another lesson. We are challenged to bring the message of God's saving grace to the whole world.

For meditation
Woman, you have great faith. Let your wish be granted. (Mt 15:28)

Twenty-First Sunday in Ordinary Time
Gospel reading: Matthew 16:13-20

Reflection

The people who knew Jesus, including some of his disciples, believed him to be a great prophet, such as John the Baptist, Elijah, Jeremiah or one of the other prophets. But, when asked by Jesus to offer an opinion about his identity, Peter said: 'You are the Christ, the Son of the living God' (Mt 16:16).

Jesus made clear that this was a particular grace from God which allowed Peter, from among all the apostles and disciples, to discern the true identity of Jesus. In this way, Peter announced his belief that Jesus was the promised Messiah who had come to deliver God's people from the bondage of sin. Jesus was much more than a prophet, and Peter was divinely inspired to acknowledge this truth.

The public manifestation of Peter's faith in Jesus as the Christ, the Anointed One, was immediately rewarded by Christ who wanted Peter to know two facts. First, he had been especially blessed by God in being given this knowledge.

Secondly, Peter was given a singularly important role in the infant Church: 'You are Peter, and on this rock I will build my Church. And the gates of the underworld can never hold out against it. I will give you the keys of the kingdom of heaven: whatever you bind on earth shall be considered bound in heaven; whatever you loose on earth shall be considered loosed in heaven' (Mt 16:18-19).

Thus we find an instance of the Old Testament custom of changing names at a pivotal moment in the salvation history of the Chosen People. For example, in the case of Abraham, we read: 'You shall no longer be called Abram; your name shall be Abraham, for I make you father of a multitude of nations' (Gen 17:5). Similarly, regarding Jacob, we read: 'Your name shall no longer be Jacob, but Israel' (Gen 32:28).

Jesus changed Simon's name to Peter (meaning rock), explaining that it would be upon the rock of Peter that the Church would be built. Just as the Father had given Peter special insight into the identity of Jesus, so Christ now delegated his own authority to Peter and his successors

Interestingly, after giving authority to Peter, Jesus commanded his disciples to tell no one that he was the Christ. This command has been much debated because in other places in the gospels Jesus did not deny that he was the Messiah, most famously when speaking with the Samaritan woman at the well. When she mentioned the Messiah, Jesus replied: 'I who am speaking to you, I am he' (Jn 4:25).

There are several reasons why Jesus instructed Peter and the others to remain silent about his identity, not least to protect them from harm because, as subsequent verses indicate, they had not yet been prepared by Jesus for the persecutions to come. However, the important lesson for us in these verses is that here we are reminded of the supernatural origins of the papacy. Peter and those popes who followed him have their crucial leadership role in the Church by divine mandate.

Therefore, when the Pope speaks definitively (that is, finally) on matters of faith and morality, teaching something that must be held by all the faithful, Catholics are bound to obey and adhere to that teaching. This definite teaching need not always come in the form of a public pronouncement, but applies whenever the Pope is repeating teachings that have always been accepted by the Church from the earliest days. The Pope's authority is limited, however, in that his office is one of guardianship. He is to guard, promote and teach the Christian faith but he is not authorised to add anything to it.

It is difficult being the Pope in the contemporary world when the teaching of Christ and the moral law often challenge modern fashions and trends. So let us pray for the Pope who is charged with upholding and defending the Church's teachings.

For meditation
But you, who do you say I am? (Mt 16:15)

Twenty-Second Sunday in Ordinary Time
Gospel reading: Matthew 16:21-27

Reflection

When Jesus told his disciples that he was going to Jerusalem and would suffer grievously there, and be put to death and then rise again, they must have been confused and distressed. Peter had been appointed the rock on which Jesus would build his Church. Now he was hearing that Jesus was going to be put to death.

Impetuous as ever, Peter remonstrated with Jesus, saying that this could not be true. Jesus was the Christ, the Son of the living God – Peter had acknowledged this earlier and Christ had confirmed it, pointing out that it was God who had inspired this knowledge in Peter. So how could the Son of God be about to suffer and die? The faith that had led to Peter's insights about Jesus being the Messiah had now deserted him.

In turn, Jesus' response to Peter's hostile reaction to his future suffering was stern, unlike his warm words when Peter had affirmed his belief that Jesus was the Son of God. He castigated Peter: 'Get behind me, Satan! You are an obstacle in my path, because the way you think is not God's way but man's' (Mt 16:23).

Jesus then described the essential condition of being one of his followers, and this condition would apply to Peter, the first pope, just as much as to the humblest disciple: 'If anyone wants to be a follower of mine, let him renounce himself and take up his cross and follow me' (Mt 16:24).

For the disciples, this teaching must have seemed incomprehensible. Even today, many people resist the idea of having to embrace suffering. Yet dealing with suffering is at the root of the Christian life. The willingness to appreciate the transformative value of suffering is a pre-requisite for authentic Christian living.

Recognising the disciples' incomprehension, Jesus sought to make them understand. He told them that, in order to gain eternal life, they must lose this life – their attachment to the things of this world. Nothing matters more than pleasing God.

Jesus posed a crucial rhetorical question: 'What, then, will a man gain if he wins the whole world and ruins his life? Or what has a man to offer in exchange for his life?' (Mt 16:26). What, Jesus asked, is more important than saving the soul?

If we lose our soul, what joy will the pleasures of this world bring us? None. On the contrary, they will haunt us throughout eternity as the cause of our downfall. Jesus reminds us, as he reminded his first disciples, about this possibility: 'For the Son of man is going to come in the glory of his Father with his angels, and, when he does, he will reward each one according to his behaviour' (Mt 16:27).

In summary, then, the reality of Christian living is that we are challenged to be fully prepared to suffer for the kingdom of heaven. We need to be clear in our minds and hearts about the central importance of saving souls. That is our greatest task while living in this world.

For meditation
If anyone wants to be a follower of mine, let him renounce himself and take up his cross and follow me. (Mt 16:24)

Twenty-Third Sunday in Ordinary Time
Gospel reading: Matthew 18:15-20

Reflection

Most people dislike being corrected and they are embarrassed if required to correct others. In addition, it is not politically correct nowadays to criticise other people. Certainly, it has always been regarded as bad manners to correct someone for grammatical errors in speech and writing, unless, of course, one is a teacher or a parent.

However, once again Jesus teaches us that, as in so many other areas of life, Christians are called to be different from others regarding honest and necessary correction of family members, friends and colleagues. Christian discipleship demands that, in the words of Jesus, 'if your brother does something wrong, go and have it out with him alone, between your two selves' (Mt 18:15). This means that we are challenged to encourage other people to cease any behaviour and change any attitudes that prevent them from living fully Christian lives and allowing their souls to be saved.

Naturally, many of us avoid conflict situations. Often this inhibits us from saying what we know to be true. Many families today have members whose lifestyles contradict the faith they profess. For example, the widespread practice of unmarried couples living together as husband and wife is one of many instances of such disregard for God's law of love. Yet, few of us are prepared to challenge, gently but firmly, our children or our brothers and sisters about the inappropriateness and sinfulness of such lifestyles.

Similarly, few of us ever think about respectfully correcting colleagues in the workplace who, for example, use bad language and are intemperate or rude in their dealings with other people. We mistakenly follow society's customs about tolerating all sorts of unacceptable behaviour instead of obeying the clear teaching of Jesus who tells us to correct one another when necessary.

He goes even further. When the person we are correcting is unresponsive, Jesus advises us to seek the assistance of the wider Christian community so that the person being challenged and corrected will realise that creating mutual respect and harmonious relationships among people is the responsibility of the entire Christian community.

This teaching of Jesus is very clear. Yet it is widely ignored. Mark Twain once wrote: 'Most people are bothered by those passages in scripture which they cannot understand; but as for me, the passages in scripture which trouble me most are those that I do understand.' Could the same be true about us?

Frequently, when we are faithful to Jesus' teaching and when we correct other people gently but firmly in spiritual and religious matters, we are described as being uncharitable. Yet the gospel challenge is to correct one another in love and with respect so that the entire Christian community, all members of the Church of Christ, may glorify the wonder and the beauty of God who has made each one of us in the divine image and likeness.

For meditation
If he listens to you, you have won back your brother. (Mt 18:15)

Twenty-Fourth Sunday in Ordinary Time
Gospel reading: Matthew 18:21-35

Reflection

Why was Jesus so insistent about the practice of forgiveness in the lives of his disciples? Peter was probably embarrassed by Jesus' answer to his question 'How often must I forgive?' Jesus told Peter to be far more forgiving than he was suggesting. Peter must forgive seventy-seven times, not seven times.

In saying this, Jesus was not implying that forgiveness could be refused on the seventy-eighth and subsequent occasions. For Jesus, there could be no limit to the number of times people would forgive. Forgiveness was to be a continuous activity and one of the central characteristics of the Christian lifestyle.

So why was Jesus so adamant that his listeners would understand how his message of forgiveness was central to his teaching and preaching? Was it because he wanted to be excessively demanding? Or was it because he knew that forgiveness was among the most difficult challenges for human beings?

It would have been easier for most of Jesus' disciples to be unforgiving because they had direct experience of oppression and injustice from the Romans, who were occupying their country, and from the tax collectors, moneylenders and religious leaders. Did Jesus want to raise the standards and expectations beyond their capabilities? The answer to these questions is an emphatic 'No'.

Jesus was uncompromising about the centrality of forgiveness because he understood human nature completely. He knew that if people would not forgive one another, and if they could not graciously accept forgiveness from other people when it was offered, then they would be unable to experience God's forgiveness. Jesus appreciated that the human spirit yearns for acceptance, sympathy, respect, companionship and a sense of belonging. None of these is possible in the absence of forgiveness.

Practising forgiveness, therefore, enables us to realise these yearnings. Our greatest gift from God – the ability to love – is dependent on our ability to forgive. Forgiveness brings healing. If there is no forgiveness in our lives, then our human nature becomes flawed. We feel isolated. We become less than human and, eventually, our dignity and sense of self-worth diminish. Our innate beauty derived from being made in the image and likeness of God is shattered. There is a diminution of the quality of human life and living.

When, as repentant people, we celebrate the sacrament of reconciliation properly (that is, we confess our sins, make reparation for our wrongdoing and resolve not to commit these sins again) we are assured that our sins are forgiven and that we will have God's help to avoid sin in the future. We all need to experience forgiveness in our lives. The sacrament of reconciliation enables us to receive God's forgiveness for our sins. We become whole human beings again, capable of tremendous love and sacrifice. Is it any wonder, then, that Jesus insisted on forgiveness among his followers?

For meditation
And in his anger the master handed him over to the torturers till he should pay all his debt. And that is how my heavenly Father will deal with you unless you each forgive your brother from your heart. (Mt 18:34-35)

Twenty-Fifth Sunday in Ordinary Time
Gospel reading: Matthew 20:1-16

Reflection
Sometimes we question God's dealings with other people because they seem to receive better treatment from him than we think they deserve. They do not measure up to our often impossible standards. They may be lazy and unreliable. Perhaps they argue and fight constantly. Or they may not have our talents and skills. Consequently, in our opinion, they are unworthy of any favour or special status. So why would God treat them differently?

Ironically, as much as we want God to be involved in our lives and as much as we wish to be part of the kingdom of heaven, we do not always want to let God be God. Instead, we want God to be God as we would choose, relating to people on our terms and influenced by our prejudices and biases.

Fortunately, however, God's ways are very different from our ways. Unlike many of us, God is not envious or spiteful. He does not have a 'pecking order', placing some people at the top and relegating others to the bottom. God has no favourites. As far as God is concerned, everyone has a unique dignity and equal worth.

It can be very difficult to appreciate that, with God, all people are special. Because everyone is important, God's generosity is marvellous and God's mercy is limitless. That is how God chooses to be God and we are challenged to respect God's will. After all, God is our Creator and we are God's creatures. God has rights too and these rights demand that we let God be God.

The lesson of the parable of the landowner hiring workers for his vineyard is that it challenges us to be grateful to God for what he gives us, and exhorts us to avoid feeling cheated and complaining about the seeming good luck and better fortunes of other people. Also, if we believe that we are made in the image and likeness of God then we need to imitate his generosity and compassion in our behaviour towards other people. Rather than applying human standards to God, we need to apply God's standards to ourselves.

The Good News is that God's love and mercy are available to

all, saints and sinners alike. When we are privileged to know that God loves us in all circumstances and saves us from our sins, why would we permit rivalry to emerge between ourselves and others whom God treats differently from how we treat them? Is it not sufficient to be assured that our eternal destiny with God is secure because of our faithfulness to Christ's great commandment, without being jealous and resentful of other sinners' opportunities for salvation?

When God is generous and merciful to other people, he is not being unfair to us. He is simply being God. Our understanding of God, then, needs to change and we need to let God be God.

For meditation
Why be envious because I am generous? (Mt 20:15)

Twenty-Sixth Sunday in Ordinary Time
Gospel reading: Matthew 21:28-32

Reflection
I know a man who thinks that he fools people easily, especially his supervisor at work. Whenever he is asked to do a task, he says 'Yes' immediately but quickly ignores the request. He tries to be popular by creating the impression that he is obliging and dedicated. In reality, however, he has no commitment to work.

His colleagues sometimes disagree with the supervisor, but at least they are honest. While this man initially impressed the supervisor and his colleagues because of his apparent willingness to do what he was asked to do, his credibility diminished when they realised that he was not a man of his word. We all know people who are like that. We may be like that ourselves!

Our word matters greatly in our relationships, whether in our family or at work or among our friends or with God. When we do not have our word, then we have nothing because we cannot be trusted with even the smallest responsibility. We become unreliable, like the second son in the gospel parable about the father asking his two sons to work in his vineyard. The father depended on him. But he assumed that he could easily fool his father. His word was meaningless and he lacked sincerity.

Dependability is a desirable character trait for all genuine Christians. Otherwise, people are wasting their time with us. God depends on each one of us to help him achieve his plan for the salvation of all people, just as the father in the gospel parable depended on his two sons.

The parable teaches us that it was the first son, who initially said 'No' but then thought better of it, who actually did what the father requested. That son had undergone conversion. He had the honesty and the humility to realise his mistake and to change his decision. He became reliable.

Perhaps too often we are like the second son who initially said 'Yes' to his father's request, and then quickly ignored the request. We easily say 'Yes' to God without meaning what we say. Then our word becomes meaningless. The parable of the father and the two sons challenges us to do God's will in action and not only to concur with it verbally. This requires that, like the first son, we are continually open to the possibility of con-version in our lives and that we are honest and humble enough to change our decisions when we recognise that they are wrong decisions, especially in matters relating to our salvation and the salvation of others.

Are we people of our word? How do we speak to our loved ones, to our friends, to our colleagues at work, to God? In what ways does our sincerity manifest itself? It would be good to be people of our word. Let us decide to be honest and humble enough to undergo conversion every day and to change our wrong decisions.

For meditation
Tax collectors and prostitutes are making their way into the kingdom of God. (Mt 21:31)

Twenty-Seventh Sunday in Ordinary Time
Gospel reading: Matthew 21:33-43

Reflection

The gospel parable about the landowner and the tenants of his vineyard is very challenging. On reading it, we may initially be shocked by the disrespect and aggression of the tenants who treated appallingly several messengers from the landowner. Indeed, we are reminded of the cliché: Don't shoot the messenger just because you don't like the message!

In addition, we are all aware of instances where a person who is a key person in a team or on a project has been unfairly rejected and unjustly despised by other people. Sometimes rejection happens when those people simply do not understand how necessary and vital the person being rejected is for the success of the team or the completion of the project. However, more often and more sinfully, rejection is the result of jealousy and vindictiveness. We all know such instances from work but, even more so, from sport and politics – locally, nationally and internationally.

The parable advises us about the extent to which some people will go to further their own interests. They will do anything to have their own way. They will compromise their principles. They will blatantly disregard the reputations of friends and colleagues. They will intimidate and frighten them. In their ruthlessness, they will even shoot the messenger because they do not like the message.

Ironically, the messenger is often the only person who can help them or redeem the situation, if only they would have the good sense to recognise this. In the words of the parable: 'It was the stone rejected by the builders that became the keystone' (Mt 21:42).

While this is true in our human relationships, it is particularly true in our relationships with God. Frequently, we may reject the challenging message of the gospel. We may despise those who live good and wholesome lives because their goodness is a rebuke to our conscience and we are jealous and resentful. We may fail to realise that when we reject other people and treat them harshly, we do the same to Christ who lives in them and who is their brother.

Likewise, when we reject Christ's teaching spoken to us by family and others, we also reject Christ speaking to us through them. In rejecting Christ, we reject the eternal life that he has won for us through his suffering, death and resurrection. Christ is the keystone, so often rejected, yet so necessary for our salvation and the salvation of all people. Without Christ we cannot have life with God.

The parable invites us to turn to Christ again. It urges us not to reject Christ in our lives simply because we dislike the challenge of his message. He is the keystone who establishes and maintains our relationships with God.

Fewer things are more disappointing for any of us than discovering that our efforts and love go unaccepted or unappreciated by others. The same is true about God. Let us, therefore, allow Christ to become and remain the keystone in our lives so that, through us, he may once more become the keystone in the lives of those who have rejected and despised him because they do not accept the challenging but life-giving message of his word.

For meditation
He will bring those wretches to a wicked end and lease the vineyard to other tenants who will deliver the produce to him when the season arrives. (Mt 21:41)

Twenty-Eighth Sunday in Ordinary Time
Gospel reading: Matthew 22:1-14

Reflection
Anyone who has gone to the trouble of organising a party for family and friends will appreciate the work that is involved. Organising invitations, and providing food, drink and entertainment requires much thought. Considerable effort goes into the event.

However, it is all worthwhile when a good time is enjoyed by the guests and they depart expressing their contentment and pleasure. Even if one or two guests fail to turn up, we can shrug our shoulders and marvel at their bad manners because everyone else had a good time.

But imagine if nobody turned up! Think of the disappointment, the embarrassment and the feelings of frustration. Dark thoughts would cross our mind and, no doubt, we would delete these friends from our address book and want nothing more to do with them.

Jesus, who was an excellent teacher, used precisely this scenario to teach his listeners about the Church. The parable of the marriage feast is about the fate that awaits those who either reject his Church or who refuse to use the Church properly to live in God's grace and to prepare for judgement.

The king in the parable represents God, who invites certain chosen people to the wedding feast. Not only did those invited make excuses and fail to attend but, when they were given a second chance and the king sent other servants to repeat the invitation, those servants were physically assaulted and even murdered. So it is with the Church. People often reject the Church and persecute the followers of Christ.

The parable teaches that a terrible fate awaits those who act against Christ's Church because, as the king in the parable was angry and sent his armies to destroy the murderers and burn their cities, so will God judge those who refuse to attend the wedding feast that is the Church. All the nourishment required for our souls, all the graces to be received through the sacraments and other spiritual practices, are represented in the parable by the carefully prepared dinner that the king offers freely.

In the parable, the king eventually managed to fill the venue with people 'bad and good alike' (Mt 22:10) and the marriage feast was held. But then the king saw a man who was not wearing a wedding garment and, when he asked for an explanation, the man remained silent. The king's anger erupted again and the man was bound hands and feet and thrown 'out into the dark, where there will be weeping and grinding of teeth' (Mt 22:13).

This appears to be an exaggerated response, out of all proportion to the crime of failing to implement the wedding dress code. But that is not the crime. Jesus used the popular customs and mores of his day to teach eternal truths. This time, he was teaching that not only those who obstinately remain outside his Church will suffer eternal loss of salvation but also those who do not avail of the life in Christ that is offered through the Church.

That is the meaning of the 'wedding garment' (Mt 22:12). We know the importance of dressing appropriately for various events and it is embarrassing if we either under dress or over dress for an occasion. The key event for which the Church was founded is to prepare us for our judgement before God. If we appear before the throne of God, having failed to live our Christian vocation, we will face the wrath of the King in the next world. The words of the king in the parable are worthy of frequent reflection: 'For many are called, but few chosen' (Mt 22:14).

For meditation
The kingdom of heaven may be compared to a king who gave a feast for his son's wedding. (Mt 22:1)

Twenty-Ninth Sunday in Ordinary Time
Gospel reading: Matthew 22:15-21

Reflection

It is always heartening when a bully comes off the worse for wear in a confrontation. And it is all the better if there is a comical element in the situation.

Some people might perceive a humorous element in the conversation between Jesus and the Pharisees when they were trying to entrap him by asking him if it was lawful to give tribute to the Roman Emperor Caesar. Matthew informs us that the Pharisees were up to no good. They were discussing among themselves how they could ensnare Jesus when he was teaching the multitudes (see Mt 22:15).

They knew that if Jesus said anything that could be interpreted as criticising Caesar, they would be able to accuse him of treason, although they hated the Roman occupiers and the Emperor themselves. They were blatantly duplicitous and were shameless in their plotting and planning to outwit Jesus.

Cunningly, they began by praising Jesus, telling him that he was a truthful preacher and that he taught God's will. Therefore, they said mischievously, they would welcome his thoughts about the issue of paying tribute to Caesar.

But Matthew revealed that Jesus knew their wickedness and, instead of answering directly, he asked them for a coin. Then Jesus asked them to look at the coin and explain whose image was on the coin, whose inscription. He was forcing them to confront the truth. When they replied 'Caesar's', Jesus told them, famously, that the answer to their question was to 'give back to Caesar what belongs to Caesar – and to God what belongs to God' (Mt 22:21).

There are several lessons that we can learn from this episode. The first, perhaps the most obvious, is that it is not only legitimate for a Christian to obey the just laws of the state and to pay taxes but we have a duty to do so. We have this example from Jesus who was born into a nation that was subject to an oppressive invading regime. Here he said nothing about a change of regime. Yet he advocated being subject to the law and paying due taxes.

Another lesson from this encounter between Jesus and the scheming Pharisees is that we need to use our imaginations to take the truth to those outside the Church. Notice that Jesus did not dialogue with the Pharisees in an effort to reach some kind of consensus on the matter of whether or not the Jews should pay tribute to Caesar. He simply confronted them with the facts in an imaginative way. They were unable to refute that he was speaking the truth.

So it will be with us if we make a point of faithfully rendering the Church's teaching to those around us, whenever the opportunity arises. Indeed, we pray for the zeal to seek opportunities to bring others into the Church where the fullness of God's revelation and grace is to be found.

We know that we have a duty to render to Caesar, that is, our civic and political responsibilities. But we cannot forget that there is also a need to give time and energy to worshipping God in prayer and charitable works. That is how we give to God what belongs to God.

For meditation
You hypocrites! Why do you set out to trap me? (Mt 22:18)

Thirtieth Sunday in Ordinary Time
Gospel reading: Matthew 22:34-40

Reflection
It is always difficult when people ask us to put a list of items in order of preference. For example, deciding whether we like chocolate more than mints, or apples more than oranges, could take hours. Often in arguments, our opponents might pose a range of options which is almost impossible to answer, such as: Which is greater, your love for your spouse or your love for your children?

This is what the Pharisees thought they were doing when one of them, a doctor of the law, asked Jesus: 'Which is the greatest commandment of the Law?' (Mt 22:36). We learn that, in asking this question, the Pharisee was trying to disconcert Jesus. So the Pharisees were hoping that, somehow, Jesus would make a mistake and say something that was incompatible with and offensive to the Jewish religion. Then they could use that against him.

They were jealous of his popularity with the crowds and they knew that they were dealing with a formidable teacher who could quote and explain the scriptures expertly. Surely now, they were thinking, Jesus would fall into the error of belittling at least some of God's commandments by exalting one over another? We have probably all been in situations like this in discussions and debates, when we have been hard pressed to offer a satisfactory answer without compromising the faith or moral teaching in some way.

Jesus' reply was simple and direct. First, he emphasised the first and greatest commandment to love God with our whole heart, soul and mind. Nobody could argue against that. The Pharisees must then have been waiting, hoping that a mistake was imminent.

Then Jesus added that the second commandment is like the first: 'You must love your neighbour as yourself' (Mt 22:39). Next Jesus achieved a masterstroke. Instead of leaving it at that and, perhaps, allowing the criticism that the other commandments (forbidding theft, murder and adultery) are not so important, he added: 'On these two commandments hang the whole Law and the Prophets too' (Mt 22:40).

The cunning Pharisees must have been dejected. Not only did Jesus refute in advance any potential claim that he had diminished the importance of any of the commandments, but he had included all the sayings of the prophets in his reply. The greatest of the commandments, which is to love God and neighbour, is the basis for every other law and every exhortation of the prophets who, over many centuries, had spoken about fidelity to God's will.

The challenge for us is to reflect carefully on Jesus' defence of the truth. He did not shy away from the questions posed by the Pharisees, although he knew that they were being mischievous and trying to trap him. Let us resolve to answer honestly and thoughtfully the questions about our faith that are asked by family, friends and colleagues.

For meditation
You must love the Lord your God with all your heart, with all your soul, and with all your might. You must love your neighbour as yourself. (Mt 22:37, 39)

Thirty-First Sunday in Ordinary Time
Gospel reading: Matthew 23:1-12

Reflection

Nobody likes hypocrites. For example, our politicians are currently paying a heavy price for various expenses scandals. When they comment in interviews and discussions about the need for personal discipline in financial matters in the wake of the current global economic crisis, audiences jeer at them and are scathing in their criticism. Such hypocrisy, as it is perceived, is no longer tolerated.

Jesus castigated the Pharisees and the scribes, the respected classes in first century Jewish society, for their hypocrisy which manifested itself in a variety of ways. They laid heavy burdens on the shoulders of the ordinary people but did not move a finger to help them. Such oppression, while they themselves lived comfortably, was sheer hypocrisy and Jesus did not hesitate to say so.

Most importantly, Jesus condemned their ostentatious religious observance: 'Everything they do is done to attract attention, like wearing broader phylacteries and longer tassels' (Mt 23:5). Jewish men wear little square boxes called phylacteries, containing scripture quotations, on their forehead and left arm when they prayer, and they wear prayer shawls with fringes, which are symbolic of God's Law.

Jesus was highlighting a weakness in the Pharisees, who loved to parade the outward signs of their religion in an effort to appear holy. But the two do not always go together, and this is what Jesus was teaching when he drew attention to the way the Jewish religious leaders were portraying themselves as pleasing to God when, in reality, they were not living good lives.

The fact that they loved to gain the best places at banquets and the front seats in the synagogues was reprehensible. According to Jesus, it was not praiseworthy that they enjoyed being saluted in the market place as if they were superior to others. He said to his disciples: 'You, however, must not allow yourselves to be called Rabbi, since you have only one Master, and you are all brothers. You must call no one on earth your father, since you have only one Father, and he is in heaven' (Mt 23:8-9).

Here, Jesus was teaching the disciples that they must not be attached to titles. He obviously did not mean, literally, that no one should hold the title 'Father'. Everyone has a mother and a father! But he was explaining the importance of humility in religious service. He was denouncing the Pharisees for their love of status, and not denouncing the use of titles *per se*.

Jesus concluded this lesson on hypocrisy by stating the Christian rule which is to seek to serve others. No matter how exalted our position is, we should regard ourselves as servants of others. Indeed, one of the titles of the Pope is Servant of the Servants of God, a title first used by Pope Saint Gregory the Great in the seventh century.

Jesus began his teaching about hypocrisy by first acknowledging the cleverness of the Pharisees and scribes. Their knowledge was accurate. Therefore, the ordinary people should listen to what they said. But the people should not be guided by their behaviour because, not practising what they preached, they were hypocrites. They exalted themselves and looked down on others.

Jesus' message to us about hypocrites is simple: Do not imitate them. Instead, we reflect on his words: 'Anyone who exalts himself will be humbled, and anyone who humbles himself will be exalted' (Mt 23:12).

For meditation
The greatest among you must be your servant. (Mt 23:11)

Thirty-Second Sunday in Ordinary Time
Gospel reading: Matthew 25:1-13

Reflection

None of us wishes to be described as foolish, even if we sometimes behave foolishly. When people tell us that we are foolish we are often upset and occasionally we are insulted because to be told that we are foolish is regarded as derogatory.

It implies that we are not wise or sensible. We cannot be trusted to exercise initiative and we cannot be given responsibility. We promptly offer excuses for any foolish words and actions, after we become aware of them, in the hope that people will give us another chance. We spend our lives seeking the opposite of foolishness: wisdom and common sense.

The pivotal question is: What type of wisdom do we seek? We normally equate wisdom with mental intelligence and a high IQ. But there are other forms of wisdom, just as there other forms of foolishness. Wisdom and foolishness cannot be defined solely in terms of cleverness and academic learning.

According to Jesus' teaching, true wisdom – the wisdom that counts for eternal life with God – is not based on intellectual ability. Neither is foolishness based on stupidity. Instead, wisdom is measured by our preparedness to meet God whenever and however God comes into our lives. If we are ready to meet God, then we are considered wise in God's eyes. If, for whatever reasons, we are not ready to meet God, then we are foolish. This type of foolishness is more damaging in terms of our relationships with God than not being highly intelligent.

The difference between being wise (or sensible) and being foolish, from the perspective of Christian faith, is related to whether or not we are spiritually lazy. If we do not make an effort to be ready for God's involvement in our lives, we are like the five foolish bridesmaids in Jesus' parable about the kingdom of heaven. We will miss God and the grace-filled opportunities he brings. Like the bridegroom in the parable, God arrives when least expected. This implies that God comes on his terms, not on ours.

If, in contrast, we watch and listen attentively for God coming into our lives, always being ready to welcome him regardless of the circumstances, we are like the five wise bridesmaids in the parable. We will enter the heavenly banquet.

The five foolish bridesmaids were excluded from the wedding hall because they were lazy and unprepared. Thus we are encouraged not to be spiritually lazy during our earthly lives. We prepare for eternity by living holy and wholesome lives. Spiritual laziness and sin can easily become interwoven in our lives preventing us from truly recognising God's presence around us.

The time for preparation is now. Are we foolish or are we sensible? Unfortunately, it is often easier to be foolish than sensible because temptation and sin abound everywhere. But we are hopeful because we know that God's grace abounds even more.

We use this life to prepare for eternity. The Good News challenges us to be sensible and responsible. Accepting the gospel teaching may seem foolish to people with a this-worldly mindset but, on reflection, it is the most sensible course of action. Let us use life's opportunities well so that we will inherit eternal life.

For meditation
The bridegroom is here! Go out to meet him. (Mt 25:6)

Thirty-Third Sunday in Ordinary Time
Gospel reading: Matthew 25:14-30

Reflection

What type of people are we? Would we describe ourselves as predominantly adventurous or overly cautious? How creative are we with the talents that God has given us? These are relevant questions to ask when determining whether or not we use and develop God's many and varied gifts.

The parable of the talents has universal application. It is a parable for all people and for all times. It teaches us much about human nature and the numerous types of people in our world and in our Church. In particular, it invites us to reach our full human potential by using creatively the gifts with which God has blessed us.

Our various talents are an expression of God's love for us as, indeed, is life itself, which is the greatest of all God's gifts. As expressions of God's love, our talents are not intended to be hidden or to remain unused. Rather, they are meant to be developed by us as a sign that we appreciate God's love and blessing.

God does not give us talents just for ourselves. Our strengths and talents are best used for the good of other people and for the good of the Church. This is how we honour and glorify God. Unfortunately, many of us may hide our talents or, even worse, we may waste them by using them in useless and often sinful ways.

For example, we may know that we are effective communicators. Yet we choose not to use our gift of communication to convey the teachings of the gospel and the Church because we do not want to be unpopular. We prefer to remain undisturbed. Nevertheless, if we took a risk and communicated the truth we might bring another person consolation and happiness. Ultimately we might be God's instrument in guiding that person to salvation.

Similarly, we may have been blessed with gifts of listening and patience. But if we do not use these talents to bring peace and harmony to troubled relationships around us, we are wasting God's wonderful gifts.

Occasionally, we think that other people are more talented

than we are and we envy them. Or we observe people ignoring and wasting their obvious strengths and talents – strengths and talents that we do not have – and we are moved to self-pity. We always remember, however, that God has blessed each one of us with a unique combination of gifts and talents that he expects us to use and develop. These talents vary considerably and we do not all receive the same gifts and strengths, either in kind or in abundance.

The invitation is to trust God by using and developing our talents and strengths to the best of our ability. Thus our personal talents complement the talents that other people lack and we enable them to share with us the strengths that we lack. In effect, by refusing to be creative and generous, we cause our talents to die. By using them well we demonstrate that we are faithful and trustworthy.

What type of people are we? Do we use our talents creatively or do we hide them? The challenge of the parable of the talents is to recognise our God-given talents and strengths so that we can use and develop them as we help to build the kingdom of God in our world.

For meditation
You have shown you can be faithful in small things. I will trust you with greater; come and join in your master's happiness. (Mt 25:21)

Our Lord Jesus Christ, Universal King
Gospel reading: Matthew 25:31-46

Reflection

What do we think about how we will be judged when we die and about the general judgement at the end of the world? Do we, for example, believe in heaven as a state of eternal happiness in God's presence and in hell as a state of eternal alienation (and, in this sense, damnation) from God? These may seem rather gloomy questions but they are the questions that must be asked after reading the parable about the Son of Man coming to separate the virtuous from the wicked as the shepherd separates sheep from goats.

Many people no longer believe in life after death or in the existence of heaven. They insist that earthly life is the only life and that there is nothing after death. Some Christians – who are meant to believe in life after death – query the existence of hell. They argue that if God is all loving and compassionate, then God will save everyone from the consequences of their sins and ensure that they will be in heaven. How could such a merciful God not save everyone?

However, there is a fallacy in this argument. It disregards the uncompromising words spoken by Jesus in the parable. This argument also ignores a basic Christian belief regarding free will. While God certainly desires that all people would share eternity in heaven, he respects our freedom and accepts the outcomes of our choices and decisions.

If we knowingly and freely ignore the fundamental needs for sustenance, kindness, well-being and friendship of other people we meet, we are making a statement about our selfishness and self-interest. In deciding not to respond to these people, we are also deciding not to respond to God who lives in them. We disregard those people who need our help and encouragement.

In effect, we are judging ourselves to be self-centred rather than God-centred, to be uncaring and indifferent. If such practices continue throughout our lives without repentance, we will be judged accordingly when we die. If we opt not to respond to God during this life, then why would we opt to respond to God in the next life? Thus we will be our own judges on the day of general judgement.

In other words, we are largely in control of our own eternal destiny. Blaming God or God's harsh judgement will be futile if heaven is not to be our final destiny. We will not be able to claim astonishment about our ultimate fate because we ourselves will already have determined that fate by our attitudes and behaviour during this life.

In summary, there are two basic types of people in the world: those who care about God and others, and those who focus their attention solely on themselves. To which type do we belong? Jesus taught that when we help the needy we are actually helping him. That is why when Mother Teresa of Calcutta was asked how she could touch a disease-ridden man, she said that she was not touching him but touching Jesus.

Are we ready for judgement? If we consistently ignore Christ in this life, on the Last Day he will be consistent and treat us likewise. Remember that while our salvation depends on the grace of Christ, it also depends on our choices during this life.

For meditation
He will take his seat on his throne of glory ... and he will separate men from one another as the shepherd separates sheep from goats. (Mt 25:32)

Holy Days and Some Other Feasts

2 February: The Presentation of the Lord
Gospel reading: Luke 2:22-40

Reflection

Today the Church celebrates the Feast of the Presentation of the Lord, which occurs forty days after our celebration of the birth of Jesus at Christmas. The feast is also known as Candlemas Day because the blessing and procession of candles is included in the Mass. Jesus Christ is the light of the nations, 'the light to enlighten the pagans' (Lk 2:32). That is why we have the blessing and procession of candles on this day.

The Presentation of the Lord brings to an end the celebration of the Nativity – although Christmas officially ends with the Feast of the Baptism of the Lord. In obedience to the Law, as was customary with first-born male children, Jesus was presented in the Temple in Jerusalem by his mother, Mary, and his foster father, Joseph.

Through the prophecies of Simeon and Anna, Jesus was revealed and acknowledged as the Messiah. A similar acknowledgement had occurred when the wise men knelt in adoration during their visit to the newborn infant Jesus (see Mt 2).

But Simeon's prophecy to Mary about Jesus was distressing: 'You see this child: he is destined for the fall and for the rising of many in Israel, destined to be a sign that is rejected' (Lk 2:34). The prophecy leads our thoughts away from the Incarnation, with an emphasis on God becoming human in Jesus Christ, towards the Paschal Mystery, which emphasises the suffering, death and resurrection of Christ.

Over the preceding centuries, many prophets had longed to see the Messiah. But they had died without realising their greatest desire. Simeon and Anna were truly blessed to meet the Saviour of the world, even if the meeting was tinged with sadness because of their predictions about the future events in his life. We too are blessed because we are privileged to know that we have been saved from the consequences of our sins.

Simeon and Anna used their time well because they spent most of it in the Temple praising God. There is an important lesson here for us. It is relatively easy to spend time in God's presence – simply because God is always with us. We are not required to be in the Temple or in a church or in another designated sacred space. We can be in God's presence wherever and whenever we choose and, enlivened and encouraged by God's presence, we can be witnesses to Jesus Christ who is the light of the world.

The tradition of lighting candles in our homes as a sign that Christ is the light of the world is one practical custom that we could easily initiate to focus our attention on him being at the centre of this wonderful feast and at the centre of our lives.

Finally, on today's feast, all families can learn the value of giving thanks to God for the gift of children and can seek his blessing on their lives and work. Enlightened by the brightness of Christ, let us re-dedicate ourselves to God, confident that he never abandons us.

For meditation
My eyes have seen the salvation which you have prepared for all the nations to see, a light to enlighten the pagans and the glory of your people Israel. (Lk 2:30-32)

15 August: The Assumption of the Blessed Virgin Mary

Gospel reading (Vigil): Luke 11:27-28
Gospel reading (Mass during the Day): Luke 1:39-56

Reflection

The essential message of the Feast of the Assumption of the Blessed Virgin Mary is that Mary, the Mother of Jesus, was taken up to heaven, body and soul, after her earthly life. Thus it celebrates her departure from the earth and her arrival in heaven, where she is benefiting from the fruits of the redemptive work of her Son. The significance of the feast for us is that it foreshadows our own entry to heaven, body and soul, for eternity.

Mary is in heaven because she was sinless. She said 'Yes' to God's will throughout her life, especially when she agreed to become the Mother of his only Son, and she never yielded to temptation. Her life was characterised by faithful obedience.

That is why her cousin, Elizabeth, was inspired to say to Mary on her arrival for a visit: 'Yes, blessed is she who believed that the promise made her by the Lord would be fulfilled' (Lk 1:45). That is also why Mary was able to respond: Yes, from this day forward all generations will call me blessed, for the Almighty has done great things for me' (Lk 1:48-49).

In reflecting on the Assumption, our hope is that we will also gain entry to heaven, body and soul, when our lives on earth are complete and the Last Day finally comes. But we can only hope for eternal joy and happiness in heaven if, like Mary, we believe that God's promise to us will be fulfilled and we respond accordingly. The evidence for that belief is to be found in our commitment to the gospel, which is demonstrated by our refusal to succumb to temptation and our daily 'Yes' to the will of God.

God created us and put us on this earth for one purpose: to be happy with him for ever in heaven. Therefore, our true destiny, having attained heaven through God's grace and our own efforts, is to join the Blessed Virgin Mary in glorifying and praising God for ever.

Our faith and hope in the Assumption is fittingly summarised in the alternative opening prayer for Mass on the feast day: Let us pray that with the help of Mary's prayers we too may reach our heavenly home. Father in heaven, all creation rightly gives you praise, for all life and all holiness come from you. In the plan of your wisdom she who bore the Christ in her womb was raised body and soul in glory to be with him in heaven. May we follow her example in reflecting your holiness and join in her hymn of endless life and praise.

For meditation
My soul proclaims the greatness of the Lord and my spirit exults in God my Saviour. (Lk 1:46-47)

14 September: The Triumph of the Cross
Gospel reading: John 3:13-17

Reflection

In thinking about the Feast of the Triumph of the Cross it is worthwhile asking ourselves how we might have acted if we had been present at the crucifixion of Jesus.

We would have witnessed a horribly brutal execution, normally reserved for the worst criminals. However, on this occasion, the man being executed was innocent. He had done nothing wrong. He had been popular with the crowds and people had followed him far and wide to listen attentively as he spoke to them about God's love: 'Yes, God loved the world so much that he gave his only Son, so that everyone who believes in him may not be lost but may have eternal life.' (Jn 3:16)

This particular crucifixion was the inexcusable killing of a man who, by word and example, had taught people so convincingly about God's love. Jesus had generously fed the multitudes when they were hungry after spending time with him. He had healed the sick, the deaf, the blind and the lame. A few days before he was condemned to death, he had been welcomed into the city of Jerusalem like a king. And now he was led like a lamb to be slaughtered. It is most probable that, if we were there, we would have stood like so many others, and done nothing. Or we may have joined the crowd who shouted: 'Crucify him! Crucify him!' (Jn 19:6)

Yet approximately two thousand years later, we are celebrating what seems to be the greatest of all contradictions – the triumph of the cross. We do so because the cross, a sign of failure and death to those present at the actual crucifixion on Calvary, has been transformed by the saving love of God into the sign, not of rejection and failure, but of salvation and hope for the entire human race. In a conversation with Nicodemus, Jesus had said that, to save the world, 'the Son of Man must be lifted up as Moses lifted up the serpent in the desert' (Jn 3:14). He was lifted up – on the cross.

If anyone had suggested to those who actually witnessed the torture and death of Jesus on the cross that future followers of Christ would institute a special feast day to celebrate the triumph, or exaltation, of the cross on which Jesus died such an horrific death, they would have been astonished. They would have refused to believe that it could happen.

So, then, what do we learn from this great feast day that we can put into practice in our lives? We can learn the virtue of patience in suffering. We can also learn not merely to accept suffering passively, when it is unavoidable, but to embrace whatever suffering comes to us in the spirit of the innocent Christ who endured unimaginable torture and a brutal death because of our sins. And we learn that what may seem to be a sign of failure, rejection and death is, instead, a sign of victory and triumph over sin and death.

Praised be Jesus Christ who suffered and died for our sins and who rose triumphant from the dead.

For meditation
For God sent his Son into the world not to condemn the world, but so that through him the world might be saved. (Jn 3:17)

1 November: All Saints
Gospel reading: Matthew 5:1-12

Reflection

We all know what is meant when we hear someone say about another person: 'That person is the nearest thing to a saint that I've met.' This statement implies that the person is good, kind, cheerful and helpful. It acknowledges that the person is sincere and prepared to sacrifice his or her needs for the greater good of other people. In short, it says that the person is holy and thus resembles a canonised saint.

Perhaps the easiest way to explain the concept of holiness is to say that it is the imitation of God (in Latin: *imitatio Dei*). Human beings are made in the image and likeness of God (see Gen 1:26) and are, therefore, called by God to manifest – to the extent that it is possible for finite creatures to reflect any of the divine attributes – aspects of the truth, beauty and perfection that are only properly found in God. Essentially, then, that is what saintly people do: they bring God's presence and blessing into the lives of other people.

In his various letters to the newly established Christian communities, Saint Paul frequently referred to their members as those who were 'called to be saints' (see, for example, Rom 1:7). By doing this, he was identifying the principal vocation or task of Christians in life, which is to know that they belong to God and to live accordingly. They do so by avoiding sin, which damages the integrity of their relationship with God. Belonging to God is not an achievement. It is a state of existence and awareness to which God calls us. It is a holy relationship.

Such holy relationships with God are not confined to those deceased people whom the Church has publicly canonised and included in the official calendar of saints. Canonised saints and the devotions associated with them are tremendously helpful to us in our daily living because we learn much about authentic discipleship from the stories of their lives and from their good example. Today's feast celebrates their lives on earth and their entry into everlasting life.

But we know many ordinary people who never came to the Church's public attention during their time on earth but who, nevertheless, lived holy lives and exercised a positive influence on others. They too are saints, even if they have not been officially recognised by the Church, and they continue to guide us from their heavenly home. Today we also celebrate their lives on earth and their entry to heaven.

Then maybe there are people living with or near us whose lives are already saintly. They imitate God's goodness so closely that they are saints, although obviously not canonised and still very much alive. They may not die for a long time and they challenge us by the goodness of their lifestyle. Today's feast celebrates their saintliness.

The Beatitudes are listed in the gospel reading for the Feast of All Saints. As we reflect on them, we are reminded that, contrary to much popular opinion, we will be truly happy and blessed by God if we suffer deprivation or persecution with patience and in imitation of Christ: 'How happy are the poor in spirit: theirs is the kingdom of heaven. Happy the merciful: they shall have mercy shown them. Happy are those who are persecuted in the cause of right: theirs is the kingdom of heaven' (Mt 5: 3, 7, 10).

The road to sainthood is a difficult journey – it is certainly the road less travelled – but, if we faithfully follow the teaching of Christ and his Church, we will be richly rewarded and counted among all the saints. The Beatitudes take us forward from a mere observance of the Ten Commandments to embracing the spirit as well as the letter of God's law. Saints are not content with just accepting suffering. But, through God's grace, they are happy knowing that their 'reward will be great in heaven' (Mt 5:12).

Today, we thank God for the lives of all the saints.

For meditation
Happy those who hunger and thirst for what is right: they shall be satisfied. (Mt 5:6)

2 November: Commemoration of all the Faithful Departed
Gospel reading: Matthew 11:25-30

Reflection

In the Catholic funeral rite, the invitation to prayer during the reception of the body of a dead person in the church is particularly comforting: My brothers and sisters, we believe that all the ties of friendship and affection which knit us as one throughout our lives do not unravel with death. Confident that God always remembers the good we have done and forgives our sins, let us pray, asking God to welcome [the deceased person] to himself.

These words summarise what we are doing today in gathering to pray for all the faithful departed. We believe that our death in this life is not the end of our existence. There is life after death and it is God's desire that we would be in his heavenly presence for eternity. In the context of yesterday's feast, the Feast of All Saints, our hope is that we, and all those who have died, will be numbered among the saints in heaven.

But in order for that to happen, we must choose heaven because God, having given us the gift of free will, does not force heaven on us. Thus we decide whether or not we want to be with God for ever in heaven by how we live while on this earth. If we are faithful to God's commandments and the teachings of Jesus, then we effectively choose heaven.

If, however, our faithfulness to God is less than complete when we die because it is compromised by the presence of sin in our lives, then we will not be quite ready to meet him and enter our heavenly home. We will, therefore, need to spend some time overcoming the damage caused by sin to our relationship with God. In other words, we will need to undergo purification for our sins so that we will be able to glory in God's presence.

Traditionally, the month of November has been called the month of the Holy Souls, when we pray especially for the souls in purgatory. We pray for all those who have died and gone before us marked with the sign of faith. We also include those who have died and whose faith is known to God alone. We remember especially those who have no family member, relative or friend remaining in this life to pray for them. Our intention in praying for the dead is to ask God to reward them for their goodness in this life and to be merciful to them for any sins they may have committed.

By praying for the souls in purgatory, we are helping them as they prepare to be in God's eternal presence. But they are also praying for us, helping us in our different struggles and needs. By praying for those who have departed this life before us, and by teaching our children to do the same, we are expressing our hope that, after we die, those who survive us will pray for us and for our salvation.

Therefore, we are encouraged to attend Masses and offer prayers of supplication for the souls in purgatory during the month of November and especially on the Feast of All Souls, so that these suffering brothers and sisters of ours will experience the truth of Christ's promise that his 'yoke is easy' and his 'burden light' (Mt 11:30) as they await the end of their purification and the beginning of eternal bliss.

For meditation
Come to me, all you who labour and are overburdened, and I will give you rest. (Mt 11:28)

8 December:
The Immaculate Conception of the Blessed Virgin Mary
Gospel reading: Luke 1:26-38

Reflection

The dogma of the Immaculate Conception, which was declared by Pope Pius XI in 1854, affirms that the Blessed Virgin Mary, through a singular grace from God, was preserved free from the effects of Original Sin from the moment of her conception. Today's feast acknowledges and celebrates the truth that, during her life on this earth, she did not sin.

The Gospel of Luke reveals that Mary was free from sin. We know this because the angel Gabriel addressed her as being full of grace when he said: 'Rejoice, so highly favoured! The Lord is with you' (Lk 1:28). Mary was the only human being ever to have lived who was sinless – apart from her Son Jesus.

The privilege granted to Mary of being a virgin and a mother at the same time was God's unique gift to her. Why did God choose that his Son would be born of a virgin? We read in the Book of Isaiah that it was to be a special sign: 'The Lord himself, therefore, will give you a sign. It is this: the maiden is with child and will soon give birth to a son whom she will call Immanuel' (Is 7:14).

When Mary said 'Yes' to God's request, she became the Mother of the Saviour of the world. In this way, she co-operated with God's plan for human salvation and, being preserved from sin in anticipation of the redemption that Christ would achieve by his suffering and death, she was able to devote herself completely to a life of intimate union with God. So she was the first person to benefit from what her Son would obtain for the entire human race.

Sometimes people suggest that Mary displayed fearful doubt by questioning the angel about how she could become a mother when, in fact, she was a virgin (see Lk 1:34). But by her question, Mary was simply doing what any person would do in such circumstances. Her initial response was quite natural in the face of the unknown. Significantly, though, when the angel reassured her, Mary disregarded any doubts she had and placed her trust completely in God. She could not possibly have understood how God was going to accomplish his will. But she knew that God is omnipotent and perfectly good, so there was no need to fear.

Mary's example provides a perfect model for all of us in our relationship with God. We live in a time of turmoil, even in the contemporary Church, because there are always several conflicting ideologies and viewpoints clamouring for our commitment. The daily challenge for us is to refuse to entertain them by casting aside our doubts and, instead, remembering that Jesus came into the world to save us from sin and to teach us how to accomplish God's will in our lives. Like Mary, we need to say everyday: 'I am the handmaid of the Lord, let what you have said be done to me' (Lk 1:38).

For meditation
I am the handmaid of the Lord, let what you have said be done to me. (Lk 1:38)

Appendix

Order for Gospel Reading for Sundays in Ordinary Time, Cycle A

Unit 1	**The Figure of Jesus the Messiah**	**Sundays 1-2**
Sunday 1	The baptism of Jesus	Mt 3:13-17
Sunday 2	The witness of John the Baptist	Jn 1:29-34

Unit 2	**Christ's design for life in God's kingdom**	**Sundays 3-9**
Sunday 3	The call of the first four disciples: Simon, Andrew, James, John	Mt 4:12-23
Sunday 4	The sermon on the mount (1): the Beatitudes	Mt 5:1-12
Sunday 5	The sermon on the mount (2): the salt of earth, the light of world	Mt 5:13-16
Sunday 6	The sermon on the mount (3): the new standard higher than the old	Mt 5:17-37
Sunday 7	The sermon on the mount (4): the new standard higher than the old	Mt 5:38-48
Sunday 8	The sermon on the mount (5): trust in God's providence	Mt 6:24-34
Sunday 9	The sermon on the mount (6): the true disciple	Mt 7:21-27

Unit 3	**The spread of the kingdom of God**	**Sundays 10-13**
Sunday 10	The call of Matthew	Mt 9:9-13
Sunday 11	The mission sermon (1): the mission of the Twelve	Mt 9:36 – 10:8
Sunday 12	The mission sermon (2): open and fearless speech	Mt 10:26-33
Sunday 13	The mission sermon (3): renouncing self to follow Jesus	Mt 10:37-42

Unit 4	**The mystery of the kingdom of God**	**Sundays 14-17**
Sunday 14	The revelation to the simple	Mt 11:25-30
Sunday 15	The parable sermon (1): the sower and the seed	Mt 13:1-23
Sunday 16	The parable sermon (2): the darnel, the mustard seed, the yeast	Mt 13:24-43
Sunday 17	The parable sermon (3): the hidden treasure, the pearl, the dragnet	Mt 13:44-52